AIRPORT SYSTEMS PLANNING

Airport
Systems
Planning

A Critical Look at the
Methods and Experience

RICHARD DE NEUFVILLE

Center for Transportation Studies
Massachusetts Institute of Technology

with prefaces by
NORMAN J. PAYNE and JOHN R. WILEY

First published 1976 by
THE MACMILLAN PRESS LTD
London and Basingstoke
Associated companies in New York
Dublin Melbourne Johannesburg and Madras

SBN 333 17622 7

Typeset, printed and bound
in Great Britain by
REDWOOD BURN LIMITED
Trowbridge & Esher

To
My Friends
at the
Institute of Transportation
and Traffic Engineering
University of California

Contents

List of Illustrations

Figures

List of Illustrations xi

Figures

Preface for the British Audience

The current state of the world air transport industry, particularly in western industrialized society, presents any author with a very difficult problem in writing a review of the kind attempted in this book. Air transport has changed from a certain growth business to one with a very uncertain future. This requires a major re-orientation of the attitudes of those of us who work in the business. Some of us, with difficulty, have made the change; some still hanker after the easy days of regular annual growth with the reassurance it brought as one's mistakes were lost in the annual flood of more passengers and cargo!

Richard de Neufville gives us here an analysis and commentary which is very relevant to the problems facing airport operators and planners today and in the near future. His thorough investigation of the failures and mistakes of past airport developments both in Europe and in the US is penetrating and accurate. Indeed, the facts and failures he records are well known to those of us who were involved, though few have admitted past errors.

His proposals for the future are timely in a situation in which great strain is now being placed on the industrial societies of the world, which directly affects the requirements for airports systems. He has, I am pleased to note, tersely eliminated some of the planners' favourite myths, and directed us to a real appraisal of our current problems and possibilities for future solutions. His analysis is provocative and stimulating in a useful and constructive fashion. In this book he has made a powerful and significant contribution to the future of the great service industry in which we work, and I am sure it will amply reward all those in the industry who seriously study it.

October 1975   NORMAN J. PAYNE

Preface for the US Audience

When I accepted the invitation of Professors Rene H. Miller and Robert W. Simpson to become a Visiting Professor in the Department of Aeronautics and Astronautics at MIT it was with the understanding I would bring some work-a-day problems of airport planning, design, operations and management into the classroom to interface with Academia.

It was hoped on both sides that my prior years of practical experience as Director of Aviation for the Port of New York Authority (now the Port Authority of New York and New Jersey) would be of interest to students and would provide grist for the academic mill in its search for new and better ways to do things.

From my point of view these objectives have been and are being realized. One of the principal focal points of this interface has been the opportunity to work closely with Professor Richard de Neufville in designing, laying out and sharing the teaching of graduate courses in the planning and design of airport systems, and airport operation and management.

Professor de Neufville has had an excellent batting record in the realization of the projections contained in his earlier writings on such basic issues in airport planning as the utility of mobile lounges, the viability of satellite airports and the practicalities of airport access. He stimulates the profession by asking vital, innovative questions and by pointing to practical solutions and desirable approaches when simple solutions are not possible.

This present work consolidates the earlier expositions and critically examines techniques and practices in additional areas involving forecasting, terminal configuration and systems planning.

In recommending solutions and approaches to these questions, Professor de Neufville brings into play his unique point of view as an academic systems analyst combined with his not inconsiderable practical and international experience.

It is his hope and mine that this work will enable future airport planners to recognize problems and what has to be done about them while there is still time to do it!

October 1975   JOHN R. WILEY

1 The Challenge and the Issues

A. The Challenge

Worldwide, air travel can be expected to increase substantially in the decades ahead. Barring catastrophe, it quite possibly will be three to ten times greater by the end of the century than it is in 1976. These projections imply no more than an average annual rate of growth of 5–10 percent. A threefold increase in twenty years only requires that air travel keep pace with the historical expansion of national economies and international trade – a fairly conservative assumption. A tenfold increase in the same period, large as it seems, is comparable to the increase in the number of air travelers and shipments in air cargo in the generation after the Second World War.[1] The larger rate of growth may even be the more likely one. It is, of course, quite impossible to know what the actual development will be, but that is not our concern for the moment. The immediate fact is that significant increases in air traffic will occur, and will require large investments in airports.

The rate of growth in the use of air transport will differ from country to country. As with other innovations that people like, such as telephones, automobiles, and television sets, the market for air transport passes through several stages. First, slow diffusion marks the introduction of the product and its use by the most affluent and innovative sections of society. Broad price reductions occur next as manufacturers gain experience and begin mass production. Rapid expansion then typically follows when people can commonly afford the product or when the community decides to promote its wide use. Finally, growth slows and relative stagnation sets in when people are using as much of the product as they want at the price. The timing of these stages naturally depends on the economic development and societal objectives of any country. For North America and Europe, for example, it is quite possible that long-term stagnation of the rate of growth of air travel has already set in. But in other populous areas, such as the Arab countries, Latin America, and China, the period of rapid expansion in the use of air transport may be just beginning.

New airports will be required wherever rapid growth is sustained. Existing facilities at airports can rarely cope with a tenfold increase in activity. When traffic increased like that in Europe and North America, practically every city either built a completely new airport or totally rebuilt one at an existing site. We can expect the same to happen at future centers of development. Already major new airports are being constructed or planned for Rio de Janeiro, Teheran, Osaka and Mexico City.

A different – but equally substantial – expansion can be expected in Western Europe and North America. Here, the period of rapid increase in air traffic and of building totally new airports may have passed. But the volume of air travel is now so large that even modest growth calls for major investments. A 3 percent increase at New York or London, for example, requires facilities for about half a million more passengers – as many as might be handled by a fair-sized airport. Taken together, such additions to airport capacity in the United States alone may cost as much as $1 billion a year, or about as much as the total cost of constructing the huge airport at Dallas/Fort Worth.[2]

The challenge is: how can we accommodate this expansion in the most rational and humane way? We want to be rational in anticipating the requests for service, in choosing the right combinations of facilities to serve different kinds of traffic, and in using resources efficiently. We want to be humane in understanding and mediating the conflicting demands for various services in air transport, in channeling growth so as to preserve the environment, and in meeting different societal objectives.

Responding to this challenge is far from easy. The traditional approaches to airport planning and the traditional solutions are no longer sufficient. We can no longer simply plan to build new airports, as we have in the past. In many areas, the objections to noise and environmental damage may prevent this. We will thus have to learn how to provide greater service by facilitating more intensive use of facilities through better management and reorganization of operations. Even where construction may be possible, we must recognize the political pressures that surround the evolution of air transport.

Airports are part of a complex economic and social system. Like highways and other forms of transport, they constitute important elements of the infrastructure of a nation. To the extent that they influence the pattern and speed of regional development, a purely technical approach to their design is inadequate. If transport planning is to be responsive to the aspirations of a country, it must be sensitive to prevailing cultural values and social desires. Subtle interactions exist between the public and the design of any airport. They will determine both the nature and location of the demand for airport services and, consequently, the role, size and form of the airport itself. We will, therefore, also have to learn how to model these economic and social forces, and how to anticipate and deal with their consequences.

B. Myopia in practice

During the past generation, airport designers have done a remarkable job of providing new facilities for air transport. These engineers and architects succeeded in satisfying tremendous, unexpected increases in the volume of traffic and the scope of the airport. The efforts required considerable imagination and courage. Designers had to conceive, design, and implement airports rapidly. They meanwhile developed undeniable skills in the construction of airfields. Unfortunately, this capability is relevant to only part of the problems we face today in the planning of airports.

Until the mid-1960s, the principal problems in airport development did concern the airfield. Increases in the speed and size of the aircraft, and changes in their operating characteristics demanded considerable attention and effort. Much research had to be done to develop navigational aids and runway lights so that modern jets could land safely, pavements of unprecedented thickness to support their impact and pressure, and procedures for aircraft to maneuver easily on and off the runways and around terminals. And most – approximately three-quarters – of the money for airports had to be spent on the airfield itself, to acquire the land to accommodate runways two miles long, to build pavements 2–3 feet deep, and to acquire electronic equipment for air traffic control.

Airport planning, as it is known today, is a distillation of the experience in airfield design. To those in the industry, the term has a precise meaning: it consists of fairly stylized routines for designing facilities at a particular airport. These procedures are supported by an extensive array of texts and official manuals covering such issues as the layout of the landing area, the illumination of runways, and the design of pavements. Numerous national and international agencies regularly keep these references current by incorporating recent findings concerning the perils of the turbulent wakes of large aircraft, the capabilities of new aids to navigation, and related matters.[3] This information is most helpful and necessary. But all this effort, which concentrates attention on specific design issues, does little to stimulate concern for the larger problems we now face.

The prevailing paradigm for airport planning has serious deficiencies for the situation today. This is to be expected. As a profession solves old problems and moves on to new ones, its methodology should evolve too. For airports, as indeed for highways, we have entered a period when less effort needs to be devoted to questions of detailed design, and more emphasis should be placed on planning the integration of these facilities into the social system.

The problems of the 1950s and 1960s, which form the basis for the current process of airport planning, are largely solved. Indeed, the new aircraft have about the same effect on the airfield as those of nearly twenty years ago. Then as now, and for some time to come, essentially all airliners will cruise subsonically, land at similar speeds, and (using sophisticated wheel carriages) exert the same pressures on the pavement. Whereas the focus used to be on the problems of heavier, faster aircraft, the difficulties now arise from the size of the aircraft, their number, and the resulting large flows of passengers and cargo.

Today, the dominant issues in aircraft planning concern the shape and function of terminals; the relationship between the airport and the region around it; and the role and future of the airport in the competitive environment of alternative airports and modes of transport. This situation is clearly reflected in projections of the US Department of Transportation:

Of the $11·2 billion in the 1972–1990 Plan associated with capital costs of primary airports ... only about 23 percent was estimated to be for airfield construction. The rest of the cost would be for terminal buildings, access facilities, parking, etc.[4]

We must learn to deal with these new circumstances and will, consequently, have to revise our concept of airport planning.

In fact, current airport planning is in great part a failure. In solving the problems of yesterday it has been short-sighted about those of tomorrow. Although it has successfully resolved some specific problems, it has floundered on many others. And while the situation is changing, airport planning as of the early 1970s has still largely been unable to face up to the fact that the uncertainty of the future requires flexible planning; to understand the competition between airports and with other transport facilities; to design airport terminals which satisfy the multiplicity of different kinds of demands efficiently; to grasp the implications of the peaks and lulls of traffic on the performance of complex systems; and to deal realistically with conflicting societal desires and their effect on the choice of airport sites.

Examples of these failures abound. As they are a profound embarrassment to their planners, they are generally not discussed or admitted publicly. But they are well-known in the industry. Let us mention a few.

(1) The plan for Dulles Airport near Washington, DC failed to anticipate how other airports and larger aircraft would erode its share of the traffic. Washington/Dulles consequently did not attract the market that was originally projected for it, and was for many years quite overbuilt, at a large cost to the public.

(2) The process for locating a site for new airports for New York City and London misjudged the nature of the politics of any evaluation of a large project which significantly harms some people (via noise and devaluation of property, for example) to benefit others. Millions were thus spent on technical analyses quite tangential if not irrelevant to the ultimate choice.

(3) The new 'gate-arrival' terminals at Dallas/Fort Worth and

Rio de Janeiro, which allow people to drive close to any aircraft, simplistically provide excellent service for a fraction of the travelers, but cannot fully cater to the variety of needs of the majority. The concept is attractive to passengers who can drive or be chauffeured to their points of departure, but it can be quite painful to the rest who may have to transfer between flights, park cars in some remote area, or use public transport.

(4) The designs for handling baggage automatically at Seattle-Tacoma and Frankfurt-am-Main apparently failed to foresee how easily queues and failures can accumulate in a system whose loads vary randomly. As of 1975, several years after the installation of these expensive complexes of devices, they still do not function.

The failures are in part due to the difficulty of analyzing complex systems thoroughly. Indeed, these problems raise so many issues, with so many alternative solutions, that we need large computers to examine the possibilities. As the British Civil Aviation Authority put it, 'On the question of practicability (of National Airport Planning) a major problem arises . . . (concerning) the number of alternative airport systems to be forecast and evaluated . . . On a national scale, the number of options to be examined multiplies in a most daunting fashion'.[5]

To the extent that this is the cause of our problems, there is hope that we can simply use better analyses to avoid future mistakes. Better techniques are, in fact, available. We have learned a great deal recently about using computers to untangle complicated relationships, to project the implications of a variety of designs on different groups, and to uncover attractive solutions. This experience, brought together as the art of systems analysis, has already shown that it can lead to significant improvements in planning and design.[6] This text suggests how we can apply systems analysis to the problems of airport development.

In a larger sense, the failures are also due to a narrowness of vision, to an excessive concentration on technical problems. Many of the difficulties described by the examples stemmed from poor judgment about individual behavior, political dynamics, and collective preferences. Such factors must be taken into account. Good planning requires that good analysis be allied with an understanding of individual preferences, social values and the cultural context. This synthesis is what we may call the systems approach. It provides the intellectual framework for this text.

C. Excessive Reliance on Technology

Technological arrogance has caused many difficulties. Airport planners have often blindly acted as if some mechanical or conceptual innovation would resolve a problem in providing the ground facilities needed to support a surging demand for air travel. In a field so closely associated with the dramatic technical achievements of the aerospace industry, such enthusiasm for technology is quite human – and forgivable – at first. There should be no excuse, however, for not rethinking the approach.

This misplaced faith in technology is most obvious in the kinds of designs that are proposed. Typically, some device or concept which might attack one aspect of a problem is naively seen as a panacea. For example:

(1) Automation was heralded as the means to avoid the spiraling costs of handling baggage and cargo, which usually requires a large labor force. Airlines and airport authorities enthusiastically installed a number of devices, but few have worked and fewer still have reduced costs. Automation in this field has mostly shifted costs from labor to maintenance of equipment and the provision of standby arrangements to cope with recurring breakdowns.

(2) Rapid trains direct from the airport to the center of the city were advocated as the means to avoid congestion on the roads and facilitate the access of passengers to air transport. Most of the plans for such service are now shelved in recognition of the fact that only a few of the passengers want to go between the airport and the center of the city, and even fewer wish to go during the rush hours.

(3) Special vehicles to carry passengers between the terminal and the aircraft were widely advertised as the way to eliminate long walks and much construction. Only while several airports were being built around this concept did

designers realize that these vehicles could create unacceptable delays and cost more than the construction they replaced.

Faith in the power of technology also extends to the planning process, to the way we approach problems. Airport planning has, in many respects, become a mechanical procedure which generates solutions by formula without any reasonable discussion over purpose or value – or even common sense. Commonly, for example, various airport planners have

(1) confidently implied that statistical analyses can determine the salient features of the behavior of passengers, and have gone on to forecast the exact level of future traffic (often quite inaccurately, as one might suspect);

(2) based decisions to expand airports upon a convoluted mathematical definition of their capacity, which was extremely sensitive to the nature of the traffic and contained hidden assumptions about the importance of time and other social values;

(3) evaluated the desirability of new airports on the basis of maximizing net benefits, a narrow economic criterion quite incapable of taking into account the crucial questions of who was going to benefit and who was going to pay.

As these examples suggest, the airport planning process has many similarities with American highway planning of the 1950s and early 1960s. Both have been highly successful at some levels and utter failures at others. And both require extensive revisions, each in their own way.

Slavish reliance on a set of techniques or standards causes much mischief. The existence of mechanical procedures obviates the need to think about what we should be doing: time is more easily spent on predetermined tasks. It is all too easy for designers to become prisoners of their methods, and to crank out proposals quite out of touch with what society will tolerate, let alone wish. Small wonder that the public or its government have rejected so many transport plans, for highways, rapid transit, as well as for airports.

Excessive reliance on technology is also dangerous because it leads us to believe in easy answers. It encourages us to think that more sophisticated machines or more complicated analyses will resolve difficulties. In reality, such 'fixes' tend to uncover or create new sets of problems. By thus bemusing us with fond fantasies, reliance on technology diverts attention from the real issues.

To prepare a sound basis for planning airport systems, we need to acquire the wisdom to recognize both the limitations of technology and technocratic analyses, and the potential contributions of these imperfect instruments. Only when we get close to reality can we hope to develop a sound strategy for planning and development. This text intends to help make this possible by providing a constructive examination of some of the 'solutions' that have plagued airport planning.

D. A Systems Approach

Airports fulfill a complex role in the transport network. The industry, concentrating on the problems of the airfield, has tended to ignore this fact. But we can never really design an airport in isolation; it is inevitably an intermediate destination in a larger trip or movement. We really need to develop plans for the airport as part of a system. Our focus should not be on airport planning, narrowly conceived, but on airport systems planning.

Airports perform a broad spectrum of services, through many different facilities and organizations, to a wide variety of users. The nature and mix of the activities is not stable: daily, weekly and seasonal peaks for different kinds of traffic aggravate the situation. The flows of traffic through the facilities, and the relationship between them, are affected by many, interdependent factors. Airports, furthermore, exist in a social and economic environment which imposes conflicting objectives and subjects them to continuing competition and even political conflict.

Airport systems planning – and transport planning generally – has to be equally rich in ideas and imagination to deal effectively with its subject. It is not credible that we could carry out this kind of task with a well-defined procedure and kit of tools. Perhaps the most we can expect, at present, is to illustrate by example how systems planning can be done.

Airport systems planning requires an approach which helps us examine the broad aspects of the problem. We need to develop the capability to identify the salient forces acting upon the system, and to trace out their implications for its performance. We need to acquire the ability to use analytical techniques which permit us to evaluate efficiently the enormous range of alternative designs, operating policies, and schedules of implementation that we should consider. And we need to foster the wisdom to integrate the analysis effectively with social preferences and cultural values. The systems approach to planning and design which the leading engineering and planning schools have been developing recently attempts to provide what is required.

This text suggests how the systems approach can be applied to airport planning by example and application to specific issues. Because of the variety of problems and situations that may occur we cannot, however, expect to uncover or advocate a single procedure.

Nor should we hope to find definitive answers to the whole or portions of this or any other transport problem. As Webber succinctly put it 'There is no one best answer to socially defined problems. There are no set solutions. There is no way to find out what's right. Indeed, there is no one right to be found'. And, therefore,

> since there are no technically valid answers to systems designs that affect social systems – no science can define human welfare . . . there can be only politically derived answers. The task of the systems designer is therefore to contribute better information, better forecasts, better analyses . . . such that more enlightened . . . bargaining can be engaged among the several competing publics.[7]

This is equally true for democratic and other forms of government. Both popular and elitist groups can have conflicting objectives which cannot be reconciled by pure analysis.

E. Themes of the book
This book is addressed to all those concerned with airports: professional planners, airline managers and airport operators, government officials responsible for decisions in the area, and citizens concerned with improving the outcome of public and private policy. The text suggests how to think through the

complex issues of airport systems and obtain desirable strategies for development. It tries to provide a guide to what questions to ask, how to organize a problem, and what kinds of solutions may emerge. The focus is on the basic questions of design and policy analysis: what is the context of the problem? How do we frame the issues? How do we investigate the possibilities? What kind of results can we expect?

The text addresses four sets of questions:

(1) What are the biases and the implicit assumptions of the industry? How do these perceptions of the problem limit the validity of potential solutions? To what extent do these views coincide with the public interest?

(2) What is the nature of the public interest in this aspect of airports systems? What questions should we really be asking? On what moral basis can we develop appropriate proposals?

(3) What are the forces and constraints which define and limit our possibilities? Which of these have the strongest effects and should be modeled most carefully? How do we structure the analyses so that we can sort through numerous alternatives efficiently?

(4) Finally, what kind of solution is the community entitled to expect? What kind of barriers exist to their implementation? How might we organize to obtain successful results?

The book addresses each of the most important aspects of airport systems in the context of these issues. We start off by looking at some of the cultural characteristics that motivate different communities: this is intended to stimulate an understanding of what kind of approaches and solutions are appropriate, where. Next, we consider the problem of forecasting overall loads on the airport system, as well as that of anticipating how these might distribute themselves among competing airports and other modes of transport. This leads us to the issue of access to the airport. We then investigate the twin questions of what configuration of terminals are best for what loads, and of how to determine the size of facilities required. Finally, we examine the evaluation and financing of airport systems.

Anticipating an audience of quite different backgrounds, the presentation is written in plain English, and uses professional terms only when essential. To assist technically minded persons wishing to pursue issues in greater depth, or wanting to satisfy themselves on particular points, numerous footnotes guide the reader through the analyses supporting the main arguments and indicate the major references in the literature. These footnotes can be neglected entirely by persons interested only in the overall discussion.

The intent is to stimulate readers to think about how airport systems should be planned. This is not a how-to book which provides the answers. Quite apart from the fact that there can be no single answer to many issues, the profession's concern with airport systems is so recent that there is still much that we do not know. Further research will, thus, undoubtedly lead to a revision of a number of conclusions. The book is an initial phase of a long term examination of the relation between technical analysis and public choice. It will have served much of its purpose by posing the questions which lead to greater understanding.

This discussion of airport systems has a wider significance for the planning of large-scale investments in transport and other activities. It illustrates how the traditional practice of design is being changed through a wider view of planning and engineering in its cultural, economic and social context. It suggests how systems analysis can assist the planning process by explicitly incorporating economic and social factors into the technical analysis, by defining strategies for development that provide a hedge against future uncertainties, and by indicating ways to compromise between multiple, conflicting objectives. The book should, therefore, also provide a useful reference for anyone concerned with transport and systems planning generally.

The material itself comes from many sources, and I am grateful to all the colleagues in the industry who have helped me bring it together. I am particularly thankful for the practical advice of professional airport planners in the British Airports Authority, the Port Authority of New York and New Jersey, and in various airlines and government agencies; and for the academic guidance of friends at the Massachusetts Institute of Technology, at the University of California at Berkeley, and at post-graduate courses throughout Britain.

2 Different Motivations, Different Solutions

A usual working hypothesis among airport planners is that they share common goals and problems. The assumption seems reasonable enough. The airlines use only a small variety of aircraft, almost all of which come from a few major manufacturers. The aircraft using the airports thus tend to be alike, and impose similar requirements for the length, width, slope and thickness of the runways, taxiways and parking areas. Passengers are also all about the same size and have the same physical needs. International regulations furthermore force air travelers to carry nearly the same amount of baggage and to follow comparable procedures when they arrive at the terminal to check in for a flight. It is therefore plausible for airport designers to feel that they all share the same difficulties and should work together toward their solution.

A number of international organizations actively sustain this sense of community, which is really unique among transport planners. The explicit purpose of these groups is to promote collaboration and the dissemination of solutions to problems of mutual interest. The International Civil Aviation Organization (ICAO), the only specialized agency of the United Nations devoted to transport, is dedicated – among other things – to developing international standards and recommended practices for civil airports worldwide. Airport operators and planners maintain close links through three organizations; the Airport Operators Council International in the United States, the Western European Airports Association in Western Europe, and the International Civil Airports Association in Western Europe and throughout the rest of the world. (These three organizations while they are to some extent rivals have now come together in a joint organization known as the Airports Association Coordinating Council. AOCI is predominantly American with interests in the Pacific Basin and in the remainder of the world, the Western European Airports Association is concentrated in Western Europe, and ICAA though mostly oriented toward Europe has recently widened its membership significantly.) Perhaps also because of the way air transport itself facilitates personal contact, airport planners typically maintain close professional relations throughout the world.

The logical implication of the idea that airport planners face the same kind of problems is that similar solutions will be universally appropriate. In this spirit the international airport associations have, at great expense, developed standard reference manuals on airport planning and design, and actively distributed them to all potential users.[1] Superficially, it would seem that there is and ought to be substantial agreement among professional planners as to the role, nature, and proper design of airports.

In fact, there seems to be little agreement about how airports should be planned. Examination of what motivates designers suggests that airport planning can only be rationally considered within the context of the cultural and historical values of a society. These forces appear so fundamental, furthermore, that they almost surely also dominate other forms of transport planning and policy analysis.

A. Do we really all agree?

Despite the strenuous efforts to maintain the appearance of international consensus, airport planners actually have deeply rooted differences about what designs are most desirable. Even though they all confront the same basic phenomena, that is, the operation of standard aircraft carrying passengers and cargo with similar characteristics, they arrive at conflicting conclusions.

For a very few, narrow topics mostly dealing with safety, nations have adopted common standards of airport design. For most aspects, however, the criteria are so broad as to be worthless. The ICAO Aerodrome Manual (that is, the airport planning guide) devotes, for example, five pages to the definition of the appropriate colors for landing lights around runways, but only fifteen words to the really crucial design of runways! Specifically, the total recommendation on that subject is

'Runways should be capable of withstanding the traffic of aeroplanes they are intended to serve.'[2] This guidance could hardly be more obvious – or trivial.

The international planning manuals are not totally useless. They are invaluable guides for various aspects of aeronautical safety, and do provide a core of technical facts, concerning the characteristics of the aircraft for instance, which may be difficult to obtain otherwise. But they provide little by way of practical advice on how to choose between the kinds of facilities, in several configurations, one could build at airports. Indeed, they could not, since there are no common international policies or understanding about such matters. Moreover, it appears highly unlikely that there ever will be any international consensus on airport planning and design.

Airport planners are just beginning to recognize their basic lack of agreement. A report on a 1974 ICAO conference on airports stated, for example, that 'Work on obtaining international standards was further complicated by the increasingly noticeable differences in interests and requirements which emerged in certain aviation regions'. In view of the practice in many countries of employing foreign consultants to copy the designs of more advanced countries, planners from these developing regions should learn as quickly as possible to recognize the variations in national perspective that may exist. They need to discriminate between the concepts and solutions which can be helpful to them and those which are not.

It is important to understand that the differences among airport planners cover all the major issues:

(1) The role and nature of national or regional planning for airports; should it force the outcomes, coordinate activities, or even exist?

(2) The decision process through which major questions, such as the location of a new airport, are solved; should it be autocratic or encourage broad public participation?

(3) The function and design of airport terminals; should they serve the convenience of the passengers, the economic well-being of the airport operators; or the profits of the airlines?

(4) The criteria of good design: are we looking for elegance, technological innovation, or pragmatic solutions?

(5) The basis for financing airports: are they to be commercial
profit-making enterprises or subsidized benefits to air
travelers?

The possible differences in perspective and conclusions
concern the very nature of the design of airports, and it would
seem difficult to discuss airport planning meaningfully without
an understanding of what these differences are and how they
occur.

Variations in the design and operation of airports are systematically associated with particular countries and regions of
similar culture. Since we know that airports of comparable size
handle generally similar aircraft, passengers and traffic, it
seems reasonable to assume that national differences are at
work. And indeed, each society appears to have its own perspective on the role of government, the function of commercial
enterprise, and the desirability of innovation. These views may
make them incapable of visualizing certain options or attaching
significance to various facts, and will certainly influence the
values they place on several kinds of benefits. In the United
States, for example, we organize air transport around private,
competitive airlines, each striving for their own profit, and place
more emphasis on economic efficiency than social amenities.
We also find it difficult to imagine how cooperative arrangements among publicly owned airlines, as exist elsewhere in the
world, might work. Such divergent points of view naturally lead
to a variety of formulations of the problems which, in turn,
can account for the range of solutions adopted in various
regions.

The notion that the character of a nation influences the design
process has important consequences for airport planning. It
emphasizes that the evaluation of new concepts and of alternative plans is not a purely technical process. We must also judge
the desirability of an innovation or a plan in terms of the
specific values and aspirations of the potential users. We should
then also be careful about what we might advise or encourage
any airport authority to do. What works in one context may
be quite unsuitable for another, not because the system cannot
operate mechanically, but because it fails to mesh with the
local requirements. Conversely, when assessing the usefulness of

foreign concepts we might wish to adopt, we should ask whether this technology or organization is appropriate to our needs.

B. National planning practices

To explore the consequences of national attitudes on airport planning, let us examine current practice in several countries. This will enable us to understand potential national biases more specifically. Any comparison of this sort can, of course, only illustrate the possibilities. The effects we observe may not be as striking or even of the same kind elsewhere. But we can at least presume that our observations provide a warning of what may occur and should be considered.

Let us look at airport design in the United States, Britain and France. These countries are quite similar, at least on a global scale: they are rich, highly developed, and endowed with traditions of democracy and Western patterns of culture. Crudely speaking, they are 'capitalist' in contrast to the 'socialist/communist' nations of Eastern Europe and the 'third world' of Asia, Africa, and Latin America. By thus limiting our investigation, we exclude the effects of fundamentally different economic structures and stages of development – which naturally may be significant – and focus more squarely on the implications of different national attitudes. As we shall see, the contrast between the kinds of solutions the three countries adopt is quite sharp across the whole range of issues in airport planning and design.

The comparison between the United States, Britain, and France is also convenient as a practical guide to anyone interested in airports. These nations dominate the practice of airport planning and design and are the principal exporters of this product. American consulting companies have been especially active on a global scale, probably due to the fact that the United States by itself accounts for about three-quarters of all air passengers and constitutes the greatest pool of experience. British firms are active throughout the Commonwealth countries and the former colonies, and the Government itself now sells advisory services through the British Airports Authority. The French are similarly active in many of their former colonies. (With reference to the subsequent discussion, it is interesting to note that the major French consulting group for airports is, characteristically, an agency of the government: the Aéroport de Paris.) An understanding of the peculiarities of their practice of airport planning is necessary to comprehend the nature of the subject. It is also vital to airport developers so that they can make a meaningful assessment of the concepts and products they are offered.

The three countries have distinct approaches and solutions to essentially all the practical problems of airport design, from the general to the detailed. These include the broad policy issues of national planning and airport location, as well as the particular questions of the design of terminals and the use of technology.

First of all, these countries have quite dissimilar attitudes toward planning itself. In both the United States and France, important governmental institutions devote extensive resources to the preparation of comprehensive national plans for the development of airports. These appear as sizeable documents which set out all major prospective investments in airport facilities in the country.[3] Despite their superficial similarity, however, these reports are fundamentally different. Here, as always, we must remember that things are not identical merely because they are called the same.

The US National Airport System Plan, for example, is a compendium of supposed aeronautical requirements that the national government compiles from local data. It grows out of a variety of ambitions and makes little effort to reconcile conflicting interests, to determine the most efficient use of resources – or even to ensure that the proposals are logically consistent! As the 1972 version indicates

> The data presented in the (Plan) ... are the results of decentralized use of uniform criteria ... Neither the ability of a given community to accomplish the indicated work, nor the availability of Federal financial assistance is considered in the preparation of the Plan. Also, the airport projects in the Plan are not ranked in terms of priorities.

The US National Airport System Plan is basically a 'wish list' of aviation enthusiasts. Projects become part of the Plan if they pass certain minimal tests concerning their suitability for airports of a particular size. There is little assurance that the Government can or will do much to implement the Plan; in fact, it explicitly denies any such commitment. The practical significance of the US Plan is that it provides a list of the projects eligible to fight for the privilege of receiving funds from the National Airport Development Program.

In France, it is quite the other way around. Right from the start, the French expect their plans to be working documents indicating what the national Government intends to do. The technical and administrative experts in the central planning agency develop the plans through extensive consultations with the governmental authorities that operate the airports and the national airlines, with the budgetary and banking officials who provide the financial resources, and with other powerful industrial and political groups who might be interested. The basic idea is to stimulate a consensus among the various authorities so that they will act in harmonious concert and carry out the plans as stated. Naturally, the plans are not always fully implemented for any of a variety of reasons. They remain, nonetheless, authoritative documents imposed by national elites upon subordinate communities.

In Britain, meanwhile, airport planning is in a period of transition, somewhat midway between American and French practice. This situation illustrates a recurrent theme in British politics: the tension between authoritarian direction and individual self-determination. The central Government retains great authority over all planning: few decisions can be made without its approval or at least acquiescence. Yet the Government often chooses to exercise this power haphazardly if at all. Until recently, it had no policy or program for developing airports, nor even an institution engaged in preparing appropriate plans; the prevailing politicians appeared to make all decisions on an ad hoc basis. The situation is, however, changing. As of 1976, the British Airports Authority owns seven major airports and processes approximately 70 percent of all air passengers in Britain; its Scottish Division runs a regional program for airport development, in effect, through its management of the four principal airports in Scotland. The UK Civil Aviation Authority is concurrently preparing regional plans in anticipation of a national policy statement tentatively scheduled for 1977.

National differences regarding the centralization of power

and the existence of any authority to create and implement
regional plans also emerge from the ways countries choose sites
for new airports. In France, the process is authoritarian with
essentially no public participation by local communities or civic
organizations. Such consultations would have little practical
significance for planners since the public at large has essentially
no means to exert political power on specific issues. The central
Government really dominates both the political and commercial
life of the country. It is the controlling, if not the sole, owner
not only of the major industries and forms of transport (in
particular both the principal French airlines and the Aéroport
de Paris), but also of the banking system, which it uses to provide preferential loans to favored activities. In France, the
President also appoints all the principal administrators of the
provinces. The government evidently has considerable leverage
to secure support for any particular decision. Typically, the
government decided that an airport should be built for Paris,
selected the site for the new de Gaulle Airport with minimal
public inquiry – and implemented its choice without opposition
of any consequence.

British practice with respect to the selection of airport sites, as
for the planning of land use more generally, is partly authoritarian and partly participatory. Officials will typically seek
out popular opinions through public inquiries or hearings, a
very democratic procedure in contrast to the French approach.
But this acknowledgement of the legitimacy of the point of view
of laymen should not be confused with popular control of the
actual decision-making. The authority to make and implement
decisions rests firmly with the ministers of the Government.
Curiously enough by American standards, the British Government can furthermore strictly limit the kind of public comments
it wishes to include in its deliberations. During the Roskill
Inquiry about the third London airport, for example, people
could only speak for the record as to where the airport should
be located; the Commission's rules did not allow discussion of
the important pertinent questions of whether any airport
should be built or if the Government's premise of requirement
was wrong! The UK Department of Trade in preparing a
national airport strategy for Britain has, on the other hand,
invited comments both on the nature of the problem and

possible solutions.[4] Public debate in Britain, furthermore, almost inevitably extends far beyond the confines of any formal inquiry.

The general British attitude toward actual popular participation in the decision-making process appears rather negative. This sense is captured by the following comment, which I heard frequently in various forms during the time the British Government asked its people to vote on whether Britain should remain in the European Common Market: 'This idea of asking the people to choose is all wrong, isn't it? It's the Government's duty to decide and if they cannot, they ought to resign.' While this attitude toward the increasing public participation in the process of decision is widespread in Britain, it contrasts sharply with the American point of view and, indeed, represents one of the traditional reasons for the American Revolution against the British.

A crucial distinction needs to be made here between the British and American concepts of how social choices should be made. The point deserves emphasis because, being both important and subtle, it is the source of considerable transatlantic misunderstanding. Formally, planning in the United States and Britain – for airports and other investments – calls for extensive cooperation between central government, regional authorities and independent interests. From the outside, the process appears similar. But a careful look at the inside indicates that the distribution of power in both countries and, thus, the outcomes of their process of social choice are not the same.

In Britain, power centers rather narrowly on the leaders of the ruling party: they directly control the administration of the Government; they can discipline legislators by preventing them from running for reelection with the endorsement of the party, thus virtually ostracizing them; they control numerous public authorities, such as the British Airports Authority, which are agents of the Government; they influence regional planning agencies which they created and can abolish at will; and so on. Naturally, it is seldom necessary for the British Government to exercise its powers; their mere existence is frequently sufficient to encourage substantial compliance with the wishes of the Government.

The decision process in America, on the other hand, is one of 'checks and balances', in which various independent levels and branches of society can veto the decisions of others. The President of the United States does not control the Congress or its members; the party leaders cannot bar candidates from obtaining the endorsement of their party through the popular primary elections; State laws frequently prevent governors from interfering in the administration of autonomous airport agencies such as the Port Authority of New York and New Jersey. By British standards this diffusion of power is perhaps anarchic, just as the British concentration of authority would probably seem on close inspection to be paternalistic to an American. The result of these differences, in any event, is that decision processes which may look similar are quite different in fact.

In the United States, the central government has no power to decide where civilian airports will be; the Federal Aviation Administration can only reject sites which conflict with other airports or are otherwise unsafe. Local governments, which can acquire and build facilities, have little power to force airlines to use a particular airport. The Dallas/Fort Worth Regional Airport Board has, for instance, been unsuccessful in persuading a major local airline to move its operations from the old Dallas/ Love Field Airport to the new regional airport. Conversely, ad hoc groups of citizens have been repeatedly successful in vetoing or otherwise blocking the plans of airport authorities to build new airports for Los Angeles, Miami, New York, and numerous other cities. In the United States, some form of public participation, or at least approval, is necessary to establish a coalition which could implement any plans for a new airport.

Further national differences exist with regard to the actual design of passenger terminals. In both Britain and France, and indeed elsewhere in Europe, economy in design receives high priority. European terminals are typically relatively small, crowded and uncomfortable compared to those in North America. (The facilities at Amsterdam/Schiphol and Frankfurt-am-Main are exceptions to this rule.) Airport authorities place great emphasis on reducing the costs of operating airport terminals. They do this by encouraging the airlines to share the use of check-in, baggage handling, and other passenger services so as to avoid duplication, and by otherwise keeping the capacity of the facilities to a minimum. The net result of these economies is that service can be slow and that passengers are often required to check-in a minimum of half an hour before the scheduled departures if they wish to be permitted to board their flight.

In the United States, both the airport authorities and the airlines stress passenger convenience. The airlines in particular try to make it possible for passengers to reach their aircraft easily, and spend freely for this purpose. They provide ample personnel to serve people and keep queues and delays down; supply special facilities to pack and ship bicycles and skis within a few minutes; and build parking garages close to aircraft stands. The concept of the 'gate-arrival' terminal, allowing passengers to drive to within a few steps of their aircraft, is characteristically American, and the new Kansas City and Dallas/Fort Worth Airports are the first examples of this design. The net result of all these efforts is that travelers in the United States can routinely check-in a few minutes before the scheduled departure of a flight, an extraordinary situation by European standards.

Americans also design their terminals for luxury and spacious-ness. The terminal being built by American Airlines in Boston in 1975, for instance, provides about 70 square feet of public area per passenger in the peak hour. With the cost of a large airline terminal averaging about $100 per square foot, it is not surprising that a US airline designing on this scale easily spends $50–100 million for its passenger facilities at a single airport. For reasons to be explained shortly, American airport planners do not have low cost as a prime objective.

Some European observers attribute this contrast in service to differences in the traffic rather than in planning objectives. According to them, the high percentage of international traffic at European airports requires much greater centralization of facilities, including customs, immigration, duty free and the like, and this inevitably leads to greater congestion and delays. But this model of the situation does bear up to close examina-tion. The concentration of passengers due to police require-ments, whether for international clearances or security purposes, does not force designers to accept the delays common in European terminals. To appreciate that this is so, one merely has to compare Paris/Orly or London/Heathrow with the international terminals at Boston or Miami. The fact that Pan American spent about $140 million on its international terminal in New York – about as much as a medium-sized airport – underscores the idea that differences between European and American design of terminals are largely due to divergent attitudes toward services.

Since British and French airport planning are similar in a number of respects, being comparatively authoritarian, elitist, and economical, it might be tempting to think in terms of two broad categories: American and European practice. National attitudes are, however, much too complex to make such simple characterizations useful. To understand what motivates planning in any country – and thus to get at the real question of what ideas are worth importing or exporting – a more precise perspective is necessary. Specifically, for example, French thought is often closer to American than to British thinking. We must learn to appreciate each country's own motivations, aspirations and preferred solutions.

Airport design in both France and the United States is similar in that it features comparatively high technology. The French are fond of sophistication, and one of their own favorite words for their designs is *astucieux* or clever. They seem to delight in attempting what is conceptually difficult or advanced. For the new Paris/de Gaulle Airport, for example, they created a double-belted conveyor which solves the extraordinarily difficult problem of carrying suitcases straight up several stories. For Paris/Orly, they developed computer systems to control and manage their passenger and cargo terminal. No one else has even attempted to automate their airports so completely. (The fact that their efforts in this direction – and indeed practically all automation – have not been especially successful is a different issue, as discussed in Chapter 7.) Automation and high technology is similarly popular in American airport design: automated baggage systems are in place at New York/Kennedy and other locations; an automated train system connects the separate terminals at Dallas/Fort Worth; and automated shuttles move people between the different sections of the terminals at Tampa, Houston and Seattle-Tacoma. Compared to the French, the American designs tend to be simpler, more pragmatic solutions making up with money what they lack in finesse.

By contrast, little automation or fancy technology is evident at British airports. Their baggage handling systems are conventional rather than automated. While airport authorities elsewhere will transport passengers to aircraft using special, expensive vehicles which can raise the entire passenger compartment up to the level of the aircraft, the British have chosen to stick with ordinary, inexpensive buses. Their planners apparently prefer to develop and introduce new technology cautiously. They shun the dramatic innovation and insist rather, that new developments be both practical and economical.

A similar concern for economic rationality pervades official British thinking about financing investments in airports. The Government's policy specifically demands that all investments in the British Airports Authority return as much as the best comparable investments in industry or elsewhere. As it turns out, this Authority has been earning around 17 percent annually on its new investments in the major London airports. The economic performance of other secondary airports in Britain is less brilliant and the obvious consequences, by British standards, is that these facilities should be phased out or should, at most, receive no financial assistance from the public.[5]

Elsewhere, subsidies are a way of life in airport construction. American airport authorities must, to be sure, generally maintain a strict commercial attitude insofar as their charters typically compel them to make ends meet. But they find this task far easier than their British counterparts in that they have access to considerable amounts of cheap money. First, they are almost all eligible for direct grants – on which they do not have to show any return at all – from the $300 million a year in US Airport Development Program for building new facilities. Second, a peculiar feature of the American legal system enables these local authorities to issue bonds on which interest received by lenders is exempt from national income taxes. This means that airport authorities can raise money to build terminals and hangars for airlines at a fraction of the market rates which others have to pay. To illustrate how this works, consider the Dallas/Fort Worth Airport, which cost $800 million. Some $100 million came from various grants on which no interest has to be paid, over $100 million from private investments in special facilities, and the remaining $560 million from borrowings costing only around $5\frac{1}{2}$ percent annually on the average. The net effect is that the airport can fulfill its financial obligations even if it earns less than 5 percent a year on its investments. The French Government likewise makes capital available for airport construction at similarly low rates.

Access to cheap money is a substantial subsidy to airports. The fact that the Dallas/Fort Worth Regional Airport Board could borrow money at around $5\frac{1}{2}$ percent, instead of the 8–9 percent usual for other businesses at the time, represents a savings of some $300 million over twenty years. This is a gift from the public. In France, the Government loses directly by lending money at lower rates than it pays itself. In the United States, the loss is indirect, through taxes which are not collected.

Access to cheap money is, in some ways, also a pernicious subsidy. By permitting airports to use their limited income to pay for much greater loans, it encourages premature and thus wasteful investments. It is doubtful that Dallas/Fort Worth would have been built so large, so soon if cut-rate money had not been available. Certainly, the Aéroport de Paris could not have afforded to build the runways for the Paris/de Gaulle Airport over two years before the opening without public assistance.

It should now be clear that the airport planning processes in Britain, France and the United States are not the same. Since the physical situations they face are similar, it is reasonable to presume that the contrasts result from fundamentally different national perspectives. Let us thus look at the character of each nation and try to relate its attributes to the different planning practices.

C. National motivations

Each nation generally has its own concept of the role of government, of what constitutes public benefits, of the purpose of commercial enterprise, and of the role of technology. We can expect this cultural heritage both to predispose individuals to particular kinds of alternatives, and to make them incapable of visualizing other options or attaching significance to various facts. The preexisting points of view will tend to shape the definition of the problems, the nature of the planning process, and inevitably the outcome itself. In airport planning at least, these influences appear to explain some of the significant differences that exist between national practices. To see how this may be, we now explore the several dimensions of British, French and American national character so that we can begin to anticipate why certain types of solutions might – or might not – be desirable for any situation.[6]

A country's concept of the public interest – of what national goals ought to be and how they should be established – is a key to understanding who participates in the decisions, what kind of evaluation will occur, and where power will lie. It generally belongs to one of two opposing notions of the public interest: the unitary or the individualistic.[7] The unitary view is that society has collective objectives and priorities, which can be quite distinct from those of its members, and which ought certainly to take precedence. The individualistic view, on the contrary, holds that the public interest is nothing more than the sum of the desires of the individuals that constitute a society. One's preference between these views depends upon the relative value one places on personal freedom and societal efficiency in some aggregate sense: neither choice is demonstrably better on logical grounds. Yet one or the other of these concepts is frequently deeply ingrained in a society.

The unitary concept of the public interest predominates in France and Britain. From Rousseau to the present the French have had the idea that the nation ought to act according to the general will – the *volonté générale*. What this might be is difficult to define in advance, but it is commonly agreed that it has no necessary connection with popular desires – the *volonté de tous*. The British hold similar views. As Burke put it, 'Parliament is not a *congress* of ambassadors from different and hostile interests . . . Parliament is a deliberative assembly of one nation, with *one* interest, that of the whole, where not local purposes, not local prejudices ought to guide, but the general good . . .'

This is not the notion of government prevalent in the United States. The founders of the United States, contemporaries of Burke, in fact, took great pains to constitute their legislature as a Congress which represents sectional and partisan interests. The national government of the United States – partially established in revolt against British autocracy – incorporates an elaborate web of checks and balances, of overlapping powers between the legislators, the bureaucrats charged with the day-to-day operation of public services, the independent governments of fifty quasi-sovereign states, and numerous other autonomous authorities. Whereas the British and French have consistently tried to discourage their heterogeneous populations, Welsh or Basque, Irish or Corsican, the Americans designed their government to encourage local interests and to prevent any single perspective from dominating.

These concepts of the public interest directly shape the nature of the planning process. The American belief that all interest groups should be able to participate independently in decision-making has two direct consequences, for example. One is that information about any proposal – without which one is virtually powerless to influence decisions – be available to all. The recent Freedom of Information Act now actually compels national officials to open their files to the public. The second is that planners should consult extensively with the public about their intentions. The National Environmental Protection Act, which describes the procedures to be followed by planners for all major projects which receive national funds, explicitly incorporates these two features. Planners must prepare detailed Environmental Impact Statements which notify the public of what may happen, must describe possible alternatives, and must hold public hearings. While this Act is relatively new, it is basically a reaffirmation of the way American society traditionally arrives at decisions.[8] In this context, it is not surprising that airport authorities in New York, Boston, Miami, St. Louis, Los Angeles and other cities have been so unsuccessful in overcoming local objections to their plans.

Based on their unitary view of the public interest, both British and French planners may consider it unnecessary, even illegitimate, to cater to private interests. As a matter of principle, the official rules systematically deny the public access to information about, and thus power over decisions. In Britain, for instance, the Official Secrets Acts – strictly interpreted – make it an offense for a civil servant to discuss even the most mundane matters. True, the UK Department of the Environment has put forward proposals for Environmental Impact Analyses which would resemble the American Statements. As with so many Anglo-American comparisons, however, we must distinguish semblance and substance. There is considerable difference between having the public legislate how the bureaucrats should behave, and having the civil servants suggest what they would find acceptable. In Britain, planners may wish to consult with the public, but feel little obligation to be bound by its opinion.

A popular view among French officials is that private interests, such as might come forward if the public were allowed in the decision process, are something to be overcome, not encouraged. A chief planner for the Aéroport de Paris put it this way: 'The positive decisions concerning the new Charles de Gaulle airport [that is, the government's fiat to build it] emphasize that public interest in Europe can still overcome private interest.' He then wondered about the failure of governments elsewhere to impose their decisions on airport locations in these terms: 'Should these failures be a matter of concern depicting the decline of a social system in which collective obligation gives way to individual right?'[9] Such statements should make it obvious why French planners see that it is right to impose their will on the public.

The different national concepts of the public interest also strongly influence the criteria for the evaluation of projects. In the United States, for example, the emphasis is on standards of performance rather than on a social optimum. It is rather pointless for American planners to determine what they consider to be the best project: they constitute only one of the factors in the decision process and are powerless to impose their preferences. The most they and other participants can do is block proposals they find undesirable. The result is that the American Government generally does insist that projects pass some minimal tests. These are minimal, indeed: the legislation establishing the US Department of Transportation explicitly prevents it from applying criteria of economic efficiency to transport projects. Airport projects in particular will be recognized as eligible for Government support if they meet specified uniform standards. Further criteria for selecting projects, such as the formulae for distribution of money, result from the play of the forces that surround the political process.

In Britain and France, however, planners tend to seek the

optimal decision. The British explicitly try to define policies and projects which maximize mathematical expressions of human happiness. The UK Commission on the Third London Airport attempted to select the best site using the utilitarian principles of Bentham: 'The interest of the community is – what? The sum of the interests of the members that compose it.' With this criterion in mind, the British have developed social cost-benefit analysis into a fine art. Every effort is made to maintain the appearance of objectivity: the focus is on measurable items, everything possible is counted, and the proposed decision emerges from the resulting sum.[10] The French approach is generally similar except that, for reasons to be suggested shortly, it typically involves more sophisticated mathematical analyses.

The purely mathematical evaluation of projects hides many important aspects of any choice, of course. Assumptions about equity are submerged in the analysis, facts on who benefits and who loses are hidden, and there is no guarantee that the result will be just. The way the British Government decided how to deal with aircraft noise around London/Heathrow Airport illustrates this.[11] The planners assigned values to the inconvenience any person would sense from a given amount of noise and then laid out 'minimum noise routes' which supposedly best served society. Quite apart from the fact that these routes in no sense minimized the noise actually produced by the aircraft, the net effect of the policy is to establish noise sewers which clobber some unfortunate people so that others may be relieved. This does not seem especially fair, but any evaluation which tries to collapse all factors onto a single scale is almost incapable of taking such considerations into account. The American decision process, which is sensitive to these social realities is, conversely, not conducive to finding economically desirable solutions.

The unitary concept of the public interest naturally leads toward central planning. It is then to be expected that both the French and the British centralize power and authority over airports and air transport, as we have already seen. In particular, both governments control their major domestic and international airlines, and own and operate the principal airports through the Aéroport de Paris and the British Airports

Authority. Not surprisingly, on the other hand, the Americans have not allowed the national government to develop any plan worthy of the name, one that might conceivably be a blueprint for what should be done. The US Airport and Airway Development Act is a typical American response to a planning problem: it establishes a national program to raise money and leaves the decisions about what shall be done to political battles between cities, states and other interests.

Where the concept of the public interest defines the nature of the planning process – that is, who can legitimately participate, what criteria will guide decisions, and where the decisions will be made – the concept of the role of the state largely determines the purpose and objectives of planning. Let us now consider how national attitudes differ in this respect, and the resulting implications for airport planning.

The tradition in France – dating back to Colbert's seventeenth century policies – is for the Government to take an active role in the development of industry for national political purposes. The ultimate goals are cast in terms of international power politics. Industry must not depend on foreign resources, thus insuring France's autonomy in time of crisis; exports are a means of influence and power abroad. Immediate economic advantage is a secondary subordinate objective. To further these aims, the Government protects French companies at home, encourages them to coordinate their activities and avoid competition, and establishes foreign markets through diplomatic agreements and political pressure. Closely associated with this perspective is the belief that quality, rather than price, is the decisive factor in international trade.

The consequences of these views are evident in French airport planning. The Aéroport de Paris is far more than an agency for managing Parisian airports. It is the Government's chosen vehicle, strongly supported financially and politically, for selling French consulting services and airport products. The Government wishes it to promote new products which – as with the Concorde airliner – are sold on the basis of their prestige and sophistication rather than their economy. This role of encouraging domestic industry and providing markets for them accounts for the multitude of innovations installed at the Paris/Orly and Paris/de Gaulle Airports. The Aéroport de Paris has, finally, in line with its general role of building French influence abroad, been the promoter and financial supporter of the International Civil Airports Association, its many publications and conferences.

The British attitude toward the Government's involvement in commerce, and air transport in particular, is rather ambivalent. The unitary concept of the public interest and the powerful socialist movement have led to the formation of national corporations in air transport, such as British Airways and the British Airports Authority. Counterbalancing this tendency, there is the British tradition of *laissez-faire* commerce and belief in the value of competition.

The results for British airports are mixed. Since Britain accedes to the European practice of airline pooling – which means that airlines operating on a route basically operate as one unit and share profits according to some formula[12] – there is little competition among airlines at British airports. As the airlines are not overly worried about attracting passengers to their flights, they have little reason to spend much money on making their terminals more convenient or attractive. This fact, coupled with their desire to control costs, leads to an emphasis on economical construction and lower levels of service. British airport planning is thus geared to providing much value for money. In a different vein, however, the British have deliberately fostered competition in domestic air transport through the stimulation of the private British Caledonian airline: this is leading to substantial improvements in passenger convenience at some airports, as by the elimination of long check-in queues on the shuttle service between London/Heathrow and Glasgow.

In the United States, competition is the rule. A fundamental tenet of American commercial policy is that the Government should actively maintain competition. The US Civil Aeronautics Board which licenses airline operations, has thus encouraged several airlines to fight vigorously for passengers on all major routes and, with only a few aberrant exceptions, has not permitted them to get together to limit frequency or quality of service. Through some quirk, the Civil Aeronautics Board has not yet allowed the airlines to compete on fares, but this may change.

The results of these policies are evident at practically every American airport. As the airlines have been unable to compete on price they have fought to attract passengers on the basis of convenience and service. Their airport facilities are a key ingredient in this contest. To understand airport planning in the United States we have to visualize passenger terminals as marketing devices. They are not designed primarily for either economy or efficiency: they represent advertising for the airlines and are prized for uniqueness and luxury. Hence the high cost of American facilities which was mentioned earlier.

Having looked at the concept of the public interest as the basis for the planning process, and the concept of the role of government as giving it direction, let us finally examine the technical style of the planning itself. Each country maintains its own perspective on technology which gives planning and its products a definite character.

In both Britain and France, the belief in the unitary concept of the public interest requires that spokesmen be established to enunciate what this might be. Both countries have thus created civil servants who are expected to define the government's view. Whatever that may be will be taken as the national interest. Since civil servants will then command such authority it is essential that they be recruited from the very best sources. The logic of this process leads to the creation of an administrative elite of great status and commanding great respect. Their planning is obviously elitist.

Government planners do not fulfill the same role in the United States. They do not, in the public mind, speak for the public interest: they constitute only one set of the participants determining what this might be. Official contributions to this debate are not required, they are tolerated. Public servants generally are thought to be useful providers of administrative services rather than leaders, and it is indicative that American parlance refers to the Administration rather than the Government. Americans do not wish to be governed and resist elitisism in planning.

The contrasts between the character of the planning process in the several countries become clearer as we examine who the planners are. The French recruit their elite, for example, from highly selective schools specifically established to attract and

cull the most brilliant students. The principal directors of the
Aéroport de Paris have, in fact, been graduates of schools like
the Polytechnique or the Ecole Nationale des Ponts et Chaus-
sées. These men (sic) have had to pass through some of the
world's most rigorous theoretical and analytical curricula. Is it
any wonder that they develop very sophisticated designs? And
since French society leads them to believe in their superiority
by indicating that they are the best students of their generation,
isn't it natural for them to feel that they can develop solutions
no one can improve on?

The British, on the other hand, select their senior administrators from brilliant generalists. Quite apart from the fact
that engineering and technology are not held in high esteem,
the British are suspicious of too much specialized knowledge.
The traditional view is that experts are to be at the disposal of
the administrators, but – except in rare instances – not among
the decision-makers. The consequences are what one might
expect: British airport planning is pragmatic, sensitive to many
aspects of the problems involved, and not aggressive about
pushing technology.

As for American airport planning, it broadly reflects the
special educational traditions of the United States. Quite the
opposite of European practice, this includes a belief that advanced education should be easily accessible to most people.
Cheap university education has been available to practically
everyone in the United States for over a century through the
so-called Agricultural and Mechanical Colleges and similar
institutions. These traditionally stress the virtues of pragmatic
skills and technological solutions rather than theoretical sophistication. American airport planning similarly emphasizes
technology without elegance, as noted earlier. It tends to
produce 'brute force' rather than refined solutions. As one
might also suspect, there is no central institution which includes
the leading experts in the field, as exists in France and Britain.
American airport planning is instead practiced widely by a
multitude of competing consulting firms, agencies and aca-
demics of varying ability.

D. A consumer's guide

Any attempt to sketch the subtleties of national attitudes,

their complexities, and rich diversity is ambitious. It is difficult just to understand other cultures, let alone to describe them fully. A thumbnail sketch can, at best, only provide a partial picture of some of the important national characteristics and their implications for planning. But this should be all we need for now.

The basic lesson is that there is no universal methodology for airport planning appropriate to all needs. Its existence is a myth we should exorcize. In addition to the obvious contrasts – concerning the climate and wealth of various regions, for example – nations have profound cultural differences which should be taken into account. Countries have distinct philosophical orientations, traditions of government, and educational heritages. These lead them to differ in their interpretation of facts, formulation of problems, recognition of viable options, criteria of evaluation, processes of decision – in short, in all important aspects of planning.

Some national characteristics seem especially helpful in explaining the variations in the practice of airport planning. These concern the nation's concept of the public interest, its policies toward commerce, and its view of technology. These dimensions at least provide a rationale for understanding the differences we can observe in planning processes and its results, and may be a basis for helping us to understand the reasons for our own preferences.

The practical conclusions to be drawn from this discussion is that concepts in airport planning cannot generally be imported or exported without adaptation. Countries which hope to export their expertise in airport planning, like the United States, Britain, or France therefore have a considerable responsibility. If they are not careful, they can use their great experience and authority to impose solutions that their clients will ultimately recognize as inappropriate. Quite apart from being a shortsighted way to do business, this would be irresponsible professional practice.

Conversely, importers of airport technology or planning assistance should be especially cautious about accepting advice and designs. Arrangements that function attractively in one context may be unsuitable elsewhere. Prospective clients may best serve their own interests by carefully examining their own objectives, consulting widely with planners from various traditions. and generally searching for solutions or approaches which most closely match their needs.

3 Guessing at the Future

Rapid change has been, and undoubtedly will continue to be a salient feature of air transport. This characteristic is important for airport planning. It is difficult under the best of circumstances to design a system which can respond to the kind of high growth in traffic that has occurred in air transport. Rapid expansion requires one to plan the design, construction and operation of facilities for conditions that one has neither experienced nor had much time to think about. And airport planning is not carried out in favorable circumstances. Extreme variability in the rate, and frequently even in the nature or location of the growth in air traffic compounds the problems associated with the stress of rapid change.

An equally important feature of air, and indeed of all other forms of transport, is our inability to predict traffic demands accurately. There can consequently be little confidence in any statements about what level of investment may be needed, at what time, to service traffic. This unpleasant fact is acknowledged far too rarely. Understandably, there is little motivation to do so. Political and institutional leaders making investment decisions do not want to appear to be gambling substantial national resources on risky projects, and naturally encourage an aura of confidence and certainty. This suits forecasters well since they are evidently loath to discuss the weaknesses of the techniques that constitute their professional expertise. The result is that practically everyone associated with transport planning more or less indicates that they can provide reasonable estimates of future traffic. Actually, they do not and cannot. A comparison of predictions and realizations demonstrates that the errors inherent in forecasting traffic volumes are systematically large, especially for air transport.

Estimates of the costs of constructing facilities to meet any level of demand are also uncertain. The real cost of any construction project, in constant dollars which eliminate inflation, is typically about one-third higher than the designers' original appraisal. It is often double the assumed budget. As described later on, experience indicates that this rule applies equally well to airports, other forms of transport, and to civil engineering projects generally. Including inflation, the money needed to pay for a project may easily be up to three times the estimates developed for planning purposes. Both cost and demand are, therefore, fraught with massive uncertainties.

Failing to recognize that forecasts are habitually quite inaccurate, the industry has failed to adopt a planning process appropriate to the real tasks at hand. First off, belief in the power of technological analyses has led many planners to use highly complex and costly procedures for predicting future traffic. Yet the resulting forecasts generally turn out to be no better than educated guesses made by knowledgeable persons. This fact needs to be brought into perspective. It is both wasteful and frustrating to spend vast amounts of time and effort on pointless exercises.

A more subtle and fundamental problem stems from planners' overconfidence in their ability to predict the future. This faith has led many to act as if they could determine the consequences of any plan precisely and could, therefore, choose the developments that would be best for any place for the next twenty years or more. These attitudes produced methods for airports geared to proposing, justifying, and implementing rigid master plans that define what projects to build almost regardless of what the future brings.[1]

Procedures of this sort led, for example, to the implementation of the massive airport at Dallas/Fort Worth, which has since proven to be such a financial and operational misfortune. The planners for Dallas/Fort Worth assumed that traffic would continue to grow rapidly and that the cost of operating their automatic train would remain low, and made little provision for altering the overall concept if matters did not turn out as anticipated. As it happened, their hopes were dashed on both counts, and their rigid master plan has left the travelers, airlines, and the region with an embarrassingly inconvenient and expensive airport.[2]

Similar procedures have existed in Britain. It is perhaps only by chance that public protest gave the British Airports

Authority and the British Government the time to avert an even greater financial calamity by deciding to stop plans to build a billion dollar third airport for London..Before that bold stroke of common sense, uncalled for by the regular planning process, the Government's transport planners spent over fifteen years asserting that their predictions demonstrated irrefutably that a new airport had to be built. They also spent considerable effort trying to define exactly in which year the airport ought to be opened, as if the amount of service that would be demanded and the cost of supplying it could be forecast with that kind of precision.[3] Both the British and American cases are examples, in their own way, of the potential cost of accepting inflexible master plans.

Instead of a rigid master plan, we require strategies to deal with uncertainty. Our inability to predict the course of rapidly changing patterns of air transport, and of the cost of providing facilities for it, implies that we need to adopt a flexible planning process. We must recognize that any investment is, in some sense, a bet against the future. It is prudent to hedge these bets. We should prepare contingency plans for the unexpected, and plan our airport developments so that they can be altered to suit the circumstances.

The most serious and thoughtful airport planners have already recognized, fortunately, the inappropriateness of massively rigid plans. Attitudes in the industry are changing. But we have not yet completely escaped the errors of the past. If we therefore do not proceed to explore and understand this history, we shall be condemned to repeat it.

To see how we might forecast and plan for an uncertain future, let us review the situation. First, let us examine the nature of the uncertainties relevant to airport planning, in particular the variable growth in traffic. Next, let us look at the methods available for forecasting future demands, and consider their inherent cost, accuracy and general effectiveness. From this we synthesize a proposal for how to proceed.

A. Rapid, variable growth in demand

Broadly speaking, worldwide air traffic increased by a factor of ten during the last generation. This is very rapid indeed: traffic has approximately doubled every six years and tripled each decade. This rate of expansion is not unusual for innovations, and is comparable to those associated with telephones and televisions. But is much greater than the rate of growth of established products or activities. Automobile traffic in the United States has, for example, been expanding at only 5 percent a year, doubling every thirteen years or so. And the overall real economic growth of a country rarely exceeds 5 percent a year for any sustained period.

This rapid long-term expansion is likely to continue for quite some time, despite recessions. Although air travel may stagnate in North America and Europe, where the demand might almost be saturated, it is still likely to increase spectacularly in less developed areas. Air travel is an expensive good that people use more as they become richer. So long as average incomes continue to increase, we can therefore expect that the use of air transport will grow significantly faster than national economies. This might easily be at double the rate of economic growth, perhaps at about 10 percent a year – averaging the good and the bad – until public demands are fully met. Since only a small fraction of the world population now uses air travel, saturation of the demand for air transport is probably a long way off.

But the growth can be irregular. Periods of extraordinary national expansion may alternate with periods of stagnation and recession. This is true even in the highly developed markets of North America and Europe, which one might expect to be reasonably stable. In the United States, for example, the total number of air passengers decreased in 1961, increased at an annual rate of 20 percent by 1966, actually diminished again in 1971 and then stayed about constant for several years.

The swings in traffic volume for individual airports can be even more spectacular. The variability of separate parts of a larger entity – of submarkets of the national air transport system in particular – can be expected to be greater than that of the whole. This is a universal statistical principle which rests on the fact that the variations in the smaller elements tend to cancel each other out when added together.[4] So we must assume that the rates of growth of air traffic at airports are more unsteady than national trends. Examples of this abound, as discussed subsequently.

Planning for regular, rapid growth by itself is already a difficult problem. The lead time between the beginning of planning and the completion of construction is easily five years or more for large projects, because of all the intermediate steps required to obtain approvals, secure financing, arrange the design, and select contractors. Wherever traffic is increasing at more than 12 percent or so a year, airport planners need to be working right now on projects to double the capacity of existing facilities. Rarely will they be able to copy the designs of others; their situation is likely to differ in some significant details. They will have little time to experiment, and will have to evaluate innovations quickly without really enough time to think about their consequences. In this environment the pressures are great, decision-makers are poorly informed, and errors are inevitable.

When wide fluctuations in the rate of growth combine with rapid expansion, the planning problems become horrendous. It becomes most difficult to build the right facilities at the right time. Serious, expensive mistakes can become commonplace if the planning process does not remain sufficiently alert and flexible. A rapid spurt in traffic can easily swamp a facility with congestion, confusion and the associated costs. Venezuela's new-found petroleum wealth triggered an unexpected, rapid rise in the volume of air cargo through Caracas/Maiquetia in 1974 for example, causing cargo to be stored on open ramps, to rot and rust in the weather, and to be stolen. Conversely, however, a slump can leave a large investment idle for several years, thus easily making it possible to waste 25 percent or more of the cost of construction on unnecessary, premature interest and maintenance charges. This was the situation at both New York/Newark and Kansas City, where in each case one terminal out of three was almost empty for several years after construction.

B. Methods of forecasting

Because the potential variations in the growth of traffic can have so much impact on the effectiveness of a design, airport planners have expended considerable effort on the development of forecasts. The methods used fall into three broad categories: trend extrapolation, statistical analysis, and technological forecasting. Each has its merits and drawbacks. Let us review each in turn.

The simplest approach is to construct forecasts from extrapolations of past trends, somehow adjusted to account for the effects of anticipated developments or changes in the environment. This is how the US Federal Aviation Administration has prepared its estimates of future traffic. As of this writing, their approach is apparently evolving toward the use of more sophisticated mathematical techniques, but its basic features still are as described.[5]

At the national level, the forecasts of the US Federal Aviation Administration generally assume that recently observed rates of growth will continue over the short run, but will eventually decrease as public desire for air travel is saturated. In the estimation of future traffic for individual cities and airports, the forecasts reflect further judgments concerning the changing fraction of national traffic that goes to a city, locally important changes in the air transport system such as the introduction of new equipment or the opening of new connections, and other factors. This procedure has the advantage of being relatively obvious about its assumptions and, thus, easy to adjust to new circumstances. It is, of course, never any better than the judgment – or educated guesses – of the persons preparing the forecast.

A more insightful, but correspondingly more expensive, version of this method is the detailed market analysis developed by the Port Authority in charge of New York's airports. Instead of considering all users together, this procedure divides the travelers into a multitude of categories. These segments of the market are defined by characteristics of the users that appear to be important in determining the propensity to travel: their age (the younger generation is more likely to fly); their motivations for the trip, as between business or holidays; and so on. This method then prepares a forecast by projecting the trends of each category and summing up the results to obtain a total for all travelers. This detailed analysis can be more accurate than a more aggregated approach, but its execution requires statistics on individual behavior which have to be obtained through extensive costly surveys.[6]

With the recognition that detailed statistical analysis may lead to greater accuracy (although there is absolutely no guarantee that it will do so), and with the availability of high speed computers to do the work, forecasting is becoming a complicated and expensive business. It is now commonplace to spend hundreds of thousands of dollars on a single statistical study to estimate traffic for large projects, such as the third airport that had been proposed for London.[7] These studies begin with specially commissioned surveys designed to collect information from thousands of individuals at an average cost of $5–$10 per interview. Next, these data are associated with hundreds of geographical zones and sorted into multiple categories that depend upon the profession, income and other characteristics of the potential travelers. Finally, the process requires all these statistics to be encoded so that they can be read into computers, and then to be manipulated to fit into complicated formulas that define air travel in terms of any number of factors.[8] The tasks are monumental. The thick technical reports are intimidating. The results, calculated to a fine degree of precision, can convey a satisfying appearance of expert knowledge. Sadly, it is all too often a false image.

So far, there is no compelling evidence that sophisticated statistical techniques provide better forecasts of air traffic than simpler approaches. Although the amount of detail involved in computerized statistical analyses could possibly provide us with an accurate estimate of how people might travel, it usually does not. One reason is that, in these analyses involving hundreds of different factors, we lose the ability to apply judgment and common sense to each element. We must instead allow the computer to apply mechanical rules to determine the influence of each factor on future trends. This abdication of judgment leads to what we may call the 'peach blossom theory of polio' syndrome: we notice some coincidence of events, as between peach blossoms and the onset of polio infections, and conclude that one causes another. Thus it is with some statistical analyses; the process would have us believe that some factors affect travel merely because of some previous correlation. There is no practical escape from this problem. While analysts could avoid totally absurd relationships from their projections, the difficulty is that most social and economic relationships at least look plausible.

A further difficulty with statistical analysis is that the predictions are sensitive to the form of the mathematical model

used. Analysts who happen to choose to work with different
equations may thus obtain quite different results using the
same basic statistics and overall procedure. Although different
specialists are often adamant about the peculiar merits of their
particular approach, no compelling logical grounds exist to
discriminate between conflicting, often arrogant claims.[9] This
situation puts authorities responsible for making a choice in a
difficult situation: as experts do not agree among themselves,
the decision-makers cannot rely upon a single analysis or
develop a firm test of which analyses may be best.

Ultimately, all forecasts are in fact themselves based on trend
extrapolations. The use of a sophisticated statistical model to
develop a formula giving the amount of air travel as a function
of factors such as national product, average income and the
like does not eliminate judgment from our estimates of future
conditions. The procedure merely shifts it from air travel to
those other quantities whose future may be equally difficult to
guess.

To avoid this dependency on rather gross judgments, statistical analysts often focus on estimating the change of traffic
caused by key variables planners may control. Specifically,
technicians find it convenient to calculate what is known as the
elasticity of demand, for example with respect to the price of
air travel, the travel time to or between airports, or other important factors. This elasticity is an economic concept defined
as

$$\text{Elasticity of traffic} = \frac{\text{Percent change in traffic}}{\text{Percent change in a factor}}$$

If the volume of traffic is insensitive to changes in a particular
variable, the elasticity will be close to zero. If the traffic
changes more rapidly than the factor, the elasticity will be
greater than plus one or less than minus one, depending on the
direction of change. The elasticity is practically always given
as a constant with respect to the variable, although there is no
real reason why this should be the case. Since the estimates of
elasticity are a byproduct of statistical analyses, this form of
forecasting shares the advantages and disadvantages of that
approach.

Technological forecasting constitutes a different way of gues-
sing at the future, one that may be most applicable to rapidly
changing fields such as air transport. The basic idea here is
that the rate of invention, diffusion, obsolescence and replacement of new technology follows a consistent pattern. Numerous
studies of the use of new technologies – and even of demographic
and agricultural processes – indeed tend to support the theory
that the growth of an item can typically be described by an
S-shaped curve with respect to time. Slow rates of initial growth
appear to accelerate to rapid expansion and then taper off
toward stagnation. Technological forecasting proposes to
exploit this phenomenon to construct visions of what might
exist in the future.

A good case can be made for the use of technological forecasting in airport planning. As the history of the development
of airports and of air transport is the product of a continuous
stream of innovations, we cannot reasonably expect that the
future will merely be an extrapolation – statistically developed
or not – of the past. It is certainly worthwhile spending some
effort trying to anticipate major technological and social
changes that might alter current patterns of use. Airport
planners for both New York and London wasted much money
and time planning and seeking approval for new metropolitan
airports, for example, largely because they failed to recognize
in the 1960s that the introduction of jumbo aircraft in the early
1970s would diminish the number of flights and, consequently,
the need for additional runways.

The process of technological forecasting emphasizes the use
of experts to estimate the likelihood or timing of critical developments, and then attempts to construct plausible scenarios
for the future. A typical exercise might try to assess the possible
opening of air routes across Russia and China which could,
with their potential for much lower fares, vastly expand travel
between Europe and Australia or Japan. A study like this could
be valuable, both to likely terminals for this traffic, such as
Copenhagen, and to Middle Eastern airports whose business
might disappear as the demand for refueling stops slackens. The
advantage of technological forecasting is that it provides a
mechanism for bringing crucial expert judgments about unique
events into the planning process. The disadvantage is that, like

all forecasting methods, it represents little more than educated guesses.[10]

C. Massive uncertainty

All the detailed work, money and expertise that airport planners have lavished on forecasting might seem to provide a firm basis for making decisions about airports with assurance. At least, that is the myth. Sadly, however, massive uncertainty remains and we must learn to deal with it: forecasts of air traffic are usually quite wrong as to the volume of traffic, its nature and its location.

A few forecasts turn out to be accurate. By the law of averages they cannot all be wrong. The difficulty is that we have no effective way of knowing in advance which may happen to be correct. One might think that one could evaluate the validity of different models by looking at how well they can replicate the past. If models could not work well earlier, there is little reason to believe they will do so in the future. In practice, however, the fact is that all serious models for predicting future traffic fit the historical record well. It is actually trivial to develop a model that does this; one merely has to try out enough combinations of variables; the laws of statistics then practically guarantee that some combination will provide a close match with the data. It is, therefore, not practical to determine the accuracy of any particular forecast or model using retrospective studies.

We can, however, evaluate the overall track record of forecasts of air transport – or of any other mode. We can estimate the range of the errors that are likely to occur. This information can be most valuable in the planning process. It provides a direct indication of the chances that proposed investments may be either insufficient or premature and unnecessary. It therefore enables us to evaluate alternative strategies of development more incisively.

As a general rule, forecasts of overall national or international traffic represent our most accurate predictions. This is because the variability of aggregate measures is less than that of their components. In this case, overestimates for some airports tend to cancel out underestimates for others, making forecasts of national traffic more stable and easier to produce accurately. Even so, the accuracy of national projections is rather low.

An idea of the errors inherent in forecasts of national trends in demand can be obtained by looking at the record of the US Federal Aviation Administration. For around twenty years, this agency and its predecessors have generated annual projections of the passengers and passenger-miles to be flown in the United States and overseas. We thus have a lengthy record of forecasts that we can compare with actual traffic.[11]

Crudely, it is even money that aggregate forecasts of air traffic six years ahead will be about 20 percent in error. The possible errors become larger as we project further into the future. Table 3.1 shows the likely errors increase by about 3 percent for each

TABLE 3.1 *Average Errors in the Forecasts of Air Traffic of the US Federal Aviation Administration, 1958–71*

Nature of Traffic	Type of Traffic	Percent Error which is Exceeded Half the Time after Each Year					
		One Year	Two Years	Three Years	Four Years	Five Years	Six Years
International	Passengers	8·0	10·9	14·0	14·0	15·1	15·8
	Pax-Miles	7·2	10·9	13·8	15·7	16·7	19·5
	Average	7·6	10·9	13·9	14·9	15·9	17·6
US Domestic	Passengers	2·9	6·2	11·2	14·1	18·3	20·4
	Pax-Miles	2·9	6·0	10·6	14·5	18·3	21·8
	Average	2·9	6·1	10·9	14·3	18·3	21·1

year further we look ahead. Figure 3.1 further illustrates the range of error and the difficulty in determining which forecast might be most reliable. Here we see that the 1965 forecast of the US Civil Aeronautics Board, which appears most accurate for 1974, was off by 20 percent five years earlier. Conversely, the 1967 forecast of the US Federal Aviation Administration, which is off by almost 25 percent for 1974 was right on target in the earlier period. Not only is there no telling which forecast is best, but it is likely that actual levels of traffic will, at some time or another, diverge substantially from the prediction.

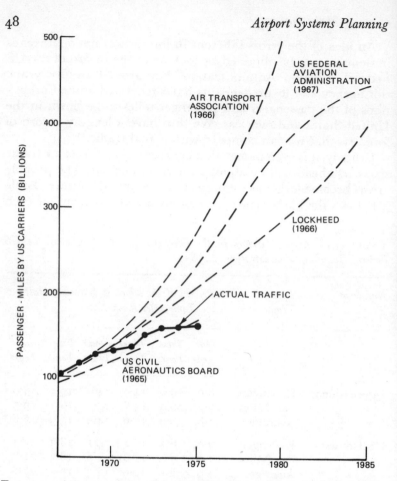

FIG. 3.1   A comparison of various forecasts with actual air traffic

The inherent lack of reliability of our forecasts is also evident in our estimates of the elasticity of demand. For example, Figure 3.2 shows the distribution of the elasticity of demand for air travel with respect to price, for regularly scheduled non-charter, long distance travelers. These figures come from fifty-nine published reports of statistical analyses of this market. The results are fairly evenly spread between 0 and −2·75 (minus since fare increases would depress travel). One result implies that a 20 percent fare increase would have virtually no effect on traffic, another suggests that it would decrease it by half. This

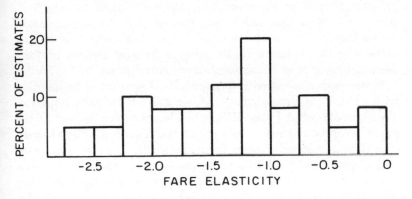

FIG. 3.2   Distribution of estimates of elasticity of air travel with respect to fares

is a tremendous difference as far as planners are concerned: it means they cannot have any confidence in their capability to predict the effect of important variables such as changes in fares. Estimates of the elasticity of air travel with respect to income are similarly broad, with a common range of 1·0–2·0.[12] The wide dispersion of these findings indicate that estimates of changes in air traffic should routinely allow for wide margins of error.

The detailed forecasts of traffic needed for planning facilities at any airport are subject to even more uncertainty than the national projections. First of all, the relative errors are greater because an airport is a component of the national air transport system. In addition, the forecasts of traffic for particular facilities at an airport result from a multiplication of projections. This multiplies the potential size of the errors. The determination of the number and capacity of the runways, for example, requires an estimate of the number of aircraft operations in the busiest hours: this figure results from predictions about the total number of passengers times the inverse of the size of future aircraft, the load factor or percent of seats occupied, and a factor expressing the concentration of traffic during the peak hours. Likewise, to determine the size of the design for a supplemental airport in a metropolitan area, we have to speculate about future patterns of airline service and of passenger traffic on the ground so that we can guess at the fraction of travelers that would use the facility. As forecasting of technological or social changes is problematic, it is hardly surprising that what actually evolves at any airport is quite often different from what forecasters anticipated.

Statements dealing with future technology should be handled with caution. A broad view is all we can realistically hope for. To illustrate what is possible, consider the conclusions of the panel recently assembled to forecast the future of large aircraft. Out of 304 aviation experts from the airlines, aircraft industry and government polled in 1970, one-quarter thought a 1,000-passenger aircraft would be used by the airlines by 1985, that is, within fifteen years or less; but another quarter felt this would not happen until at least ten years later and perhaps many more.[13] Either estimate could be right, and yet they each have completely different implications for the kind of airports we might have to build.

The case of the two major airports for Washington, DC, Dulles and National, illustrates the practical consequences of this kind of uncertainty. In 1962 the US Federal Aviation Administration estimated that the number of air travelers into Washington would grow 68 percent in five years. They put the increase in the number of aircraft operations at 39 percent, slightly less than the passenger expansion since it was known that the airlines were acquiring larger aircraft.[14] In fact, passenger traffic grew 128 percent in five years. Although this was twice as fast as anticipated, resulting in total traffic one-third higher than forecast, such a large deviation is not at all unusual, as Table 3.1 indicated. Meanwhile, however, the number of aircraft operations did not merely fail to keep pace with this unexpected growth, it did not reach the levels projected for the lower traffic, and was actually 4 percent less than in 1962! The number of passengers per aircraft was nearly twice the level planned for only five years previously: the result was a lot of unused runway capacity.

The case is by no means unique. A similar pattern occurred in the early 1970s following the introduction of wide-body aircraft into service, as Figure 3.3 shows.[15] This effect has had profound implications for many regions. For Los Angeles and Miami in particular, and also for cities such as New York and

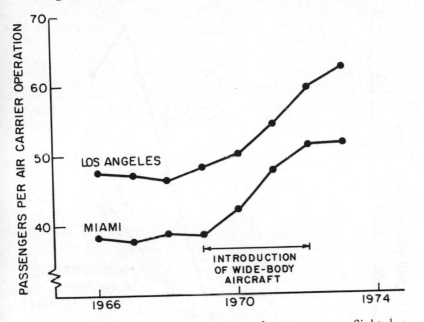

FIG. 3.3   Sharp increase in the number of passengers per flight due
to the introduction of new technology

London, it has led to a much lower demand for runway capacity
and has indefinitely deferred plans for the new airports that
seemed so critically needed in the 1960s. Similar effects can
occur almost anywhere as new aircraft are brought into service.
The resulting uncertainty underscores the fact that planning
for airports should be flexible.

Forecasts for any fraction of a city's market for air travel are
notoriously unreliable. Two forecasts for overseas travel from
New York provide an example of this, as Figure 3.4 shows.[16] It
is interesting to note how far the actual traffic can diverge not
only from the predictions but also from the bounds set on them.
As a general rule, people strongly overestimate their ability to
define the extreme possibilities. The difficulties we see here are
probably typical of what we might expect to encounter in forecasting for international charter or cargo traffic.

It should be especially pointed out that forecasts of how
passengers will choose between airports in a metropolitan area

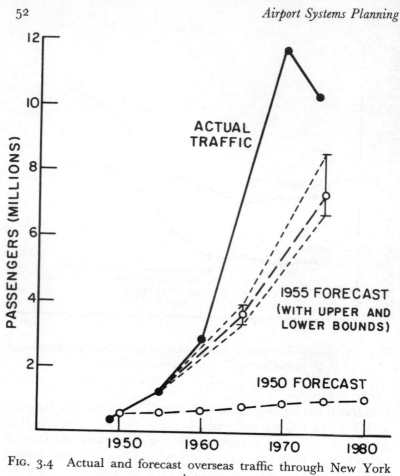

FIG. 3.4   Actual and forecast overseas traffic through New York airports

have been particularly miserable. Most of these projections have assumed that travelers will go to the airport that is closest to them either in time or distance. As indicated in the next chapter, however, passengers tend to gravitate toward the larger airports. In any event the simplistic studies are horribly inaccurate. Looking at Washington again, we see that whereas the Federal Aviation Administration predicted that Washington/Dulles would handle 49 percent of the metropolitan traffic by 1967, it only attracted 13 percent and handled one-third of the passengers anticipated.

This concentration of traffic particularly plagues smaller,

satellite airports. Oakland Airport near San Francisco has been unable, for example, to attract a substantial share of the metropolitan market for air travel despite the fact that it is closer to more of the market than the San Francisco Airport and can also provide services more cheaply. Figure 3.5 illustrates the

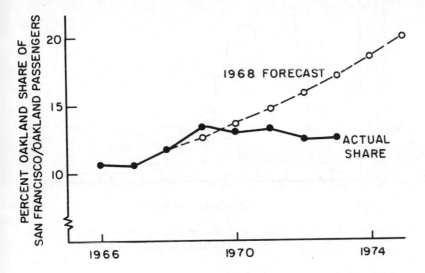

FIG. 3.5 Mismatch between anticipated and actual share of a metropolitan market for a secondary airport

mismatch between expectation and realization.[17] Experience indicates that this phenomenon is common.

While the uncertainties in the demands for service are perhaps most documented, it would be wrong to assume that the costs of supplying service and facilities are known accurately. Quite the contrary. The estimation of future costs is easily as inaccurate as any forecast of demand.

The real costs of an airport typically are 25 percent greater than the original estimate. The actual expenditures are even higher, of course, due to inflation. It is not at all unusual for the cost of a runway, terminal, or hangar to end up costing twice as much as anticipated. This phenomenon seems to be characteristic of all engineering projects, large or small, routine or not. While one might guess that the situation is worse for unique

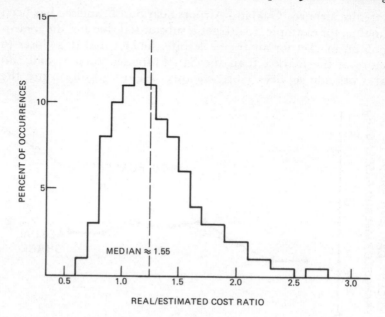

Fig. 3.6   Ratio of real costs, expressed in constant dollars, to
estimated costs for routine airport projects

activities, it is still bad for ordinary jobs. For example, Figure
3.6 shows the results of comparing the estimated and actual
costs of resurfacing dozens of runways over many years throughout the western United States.[18]

Cost overruns appear to be inevitable. To the casual observer,
it might seem that the estimation of costs is a simple matter of
multiplying quantities and prices and summing the results.
Estimators, however, have to account for all the contingencies
that might raise or lower prices, quantities or otherwise alter
the cost of a project. In practice, no one seems able to account
for all possibilities: something is always left out. Imagine your
own experience with estimates of substantial repairs to your
automobile or house.

With these uncertainties in cost, planning investments for
any airport, large or small, is tricky. It is difficult to raise the
right amount of money for a project, and to justify it economically, let alone to make it pay.

It could be argued that the gap between official projections and reality is often not a technical problem but a matter of politically motivated wishful thinking or deception. Since the US Federal Aviation Administration promoted and built the Washington/Dulles Airport, for example, they might naturally have been inclined to project a rosy future for their creation. Similarly, it would appear altogether human for people to underestimate the cost of their proposals, thereby enhancing their attractiveness. Pressures of this sort certainly surround any plan for spending large amounts of money.

All this evidence culminates in a most important lesson for airport planning. Whether the errors in the forecasts for new facilities are predominantly technical or not the practical result is the same: massive uncertainty pervades our estimates of the future. Until the happy day when the experts have demonstrated that their estimates are consistently accurate, neither the government nor the public should place much faith in forecasts. This is the fundamental setting for the airport planning process. Planning procedures which fail to recognize this fact, and which thus do not generate flexible strategies for dealing with unexpected changes in traffic, are inherently unrealistic.

D. How to proceed

To plan effectively for the future, we need to resolve two issues. One is the question of how we will go about estimating the demand for services and the costs of supplying them. The other concerns how we will incorporate this information in the planning process and use it to generate effective proposals. Let us take these matters up in turn.

In developing forecasts, the real trick for planners is to establish a process which provides much insight at low cost. This implies that the sensitivity of the forecasting models to changes in basic assumptions should be readily identifiable. It also means that we should be able to repeat analyses, both to test their sensitivity and to bring them up to date, quickly and inexpensively.

Since any single forecast is likely to be wrong in a few years, it is almost certainly wisest to develop alternative forecasts from independent points of view. Different approaches to the problem should give us a better feel for the range of uncertainty we face. In practice we might combine judgmental extrapolations, statistical analyses, and some technological forecasting. We should, in any event, spend considerable effort on trying to anticipate major technological and demographic changes that may alter the kinds and levels of service that will be demanded.

To use resources most effectively, we might emphasize simpler models. They are, first of all, cheaper and apparently no less accurate than complex statistical formulations. Simpler models are thus likely to be more cost-effective. In addition, their simplicity allows us to understand their structure and behavior, and to avoid unconscious assumptions in the modeling process with unknown consequences. Simpler models can thus enable us to understand a situation much more intuitively, and to generate and evaluate alternatives more incisively.

To bring the best information possible to our selection of investments, we should also bring our forecasts up to date during the planning process. A constant process of revision will correct the inevitable errors in the initial projection. Here again simpler models have an advantage. Complex models, with their attendant high costs for collecting and processing data, can easily exhaust a budget with a prediction for a single period. Simpler models using readily available data can, on the other hand, be used repeatedly with little effort and at low cost.

The planning process itself needs to be designed around the recognition that, since forecasts are so inaccurate, mistakes are easy to make, perhaps inevitable. We should structure the planning process so as to minimize the expected costs of unlucky choices. Simply put, it is inappropriate to rely heavily on the forecasts.

A first step in this direction is to examine all alternatives in light of the broad range of possible futures, not merely the narrow band currently thought to be most probable. A fully realistic assessment will force us to recognize just how badly any plan may fit eventual needs and will, consequently, stimulate us to take appropriate steps to avoid such futures.

An effective way to insure against disaster is to prepare contingency plans permitting easy and inexpensive adaptation to the sudden shifts of traffic that may occur. If we recognize early enough that actual loads may be substantially different from our forecasts, we may be able to prepare for them relatively cheaply, even though they might be expensive to deal with later. At New York/Kennedy, for example, the Port Authority placed extra foundations in front of the terminals, right underneath the aircraft apron, just in case they might ever have to expand the building. These piles were easy and cheap to place during initial construction, and would not have represented a great waste even if they had not been used. As it happened, they were needed, and the fact that the expansion could be built rapidly – without tearing up the parking area for the aircraft and inconveniencing the airlines and the public – was worth their original cost many times over. Likewise, it may also be wise to buy land for an airport in advance of need; the investment may not only be cheap, but even self-supporting and perhaps profitable. On the other hand, it is rarely justifiable to build major structures early; they are both expensive and impractical to scale back if traffic fails to develop.

As part of the strategy of protecting investments against uncertainty, we should also make decisions only when necessary. We should make choices on matters with long lead times first, deferring others until later. For instance, it might be wise to choose and buy a site early, but to defer decisions about construction until it was quite clear that traffic would in fact justify the investments. Conversely, the planning process should avoid making firm commitments that are unnecessary at the time, and that may be politically or financially painful to alter subsequently.

The master plans that we develop should be flexible, not rigid as they have all too often been in the past. They should provide a framework for decision-making not a plan of action. Commitments to specific projects should be made only when rising traffic or demands for better service justify the investments. Because of the ever-present uncertainties, however, the available facts will rarely support any course of action unambiguously. Decisions will thus always represent something of a gamble.

A systematic organization of all the necessary information is helpful in preparing to make these complex choices involving multiple, often conflicting, alternatives – and substantial uncertainties. This process should, furthermore, incorporate our best estimates of the probability of different futures, and allow us to trade off our expectations of future benefits and choices. Such a process, known technically as decision analysis, has recently been developed and become practical for large-scale projects.

The overall procedure suggested here appears to have worked well where it has been applied. The planning for the new airport for Mexico City is a good example of the use of decision analysis. The situation in Mexico City was similar to those in New York and London that led to such protracted, bitter controversies about new airports: traffic was rising sharply, the existing facilities were crowded and expensive to expand, and a new site was technically feasible some distance away from the city. But whereas the New York and London airport authorities mounted studies to determine the single best master plan, the Mexican authorities commissioned a decision analysis to see how each of the different strategies available might perform in any of the possible futures that might occur. (The problem involves thousands of possible combinations and could, in fact, only be analyzed with the aid of computers, such as were not available at the time of the original studies for New York and London.) As a result, they did not choose to push initially for complete development, as their American and British counterparts had done. They decided instead to buy a site, to prepare plans, and to delay construction until it became clearly desirable to proceed. This flexible strategy both allowed for possible needs of the airlines and the air travelers, and avoided unnecessary public expense or opposition, and thus obtained the support of all concerned. The Mexican plans for airport development have therefore proceeded smoothly so far where others became entangled in bitter controversy.[19]

The recommended strategy for anticipating and adapting to events is not glamorous. It does not provide officials with opportunities for making bold decisions or unveiling impressive plans. A flexible strategy may thus not appeal to political bosses who wish to leave their mark on the earth. But it does have the advantage of preventing these officials from looking like fools in a few years. A less rigid planning strategy would almost certainly, for example, have led the British Government to avoid its initial, dogmatic decision to build a third London airport, a choice they since greatly regretted. In making important national or local decisions, thoughtful caution may be best.

4 Airports and Competitors

The design of any large system for human use requires that we account for a most important phenomenon: the design itself influences the nature of the loads we must accommodate. This fact, which should be obvious, is constantly forgotten in the preparation of traffic forecasts. In planning airport systems, in particular, we must recognize that the distribution of traffic among airports and its level at any single facility can depend significantly on what services are available at which locations. If we are to provide the right facilities at the right time and place, we must, therefore, understand how the configuration of the airport system and its relationship to the entire transport net affects traffic patterns.

The construction of airport capacity, of runways, terminals and the like, does not by itself attract traffic. Airports exist to enable people and goods to reach desired destinations. These transport services are, however, also available elsewhere. The demands for airport services thus depend in no small part on the competition offered both by other modes of transport and other air services. This fact is fundamental and should be self-evident.

Yet the point deserves emphasis. There has been a widespread – and tragically costly – belief that traffic will flow naturally wherever capacity is provided. As the UK Civil Aviation Authority stated recently 'The demands for travel are in no way created by the provision of airport capacity – a lesson which the United Kingdom, in common with many other countries, has learnt at heavy cost'.[1]

There is essentially no intrinsic demand for airport capacity. It exists only insofar as air transport provides a better combination of services than its competitors. Travelers and shippers will always compare the value of air transport with the alternatives. We must therefore try to understand how the planning and design of airport systems influences this competition and, thus, the demand for air transport.

A favorable market area or an attractive destination is, of course, necessary to generate demand for transport. People will not travel or ship goods unless they can afford and are inclined to do so, and unless there is some good reason to do business or spend a holiday in a place. The propensity of individuals to travel consequently depends on economic and social factors such as personal income, the level of economic activity, and the availability of leisure time; on the value of alternative uses of resources; and on personal characteristics such as age, family circumstances and the like. The requests for transport to any particular place similarly depend upon the opportunities available there for business or pleasure and their desirability relative to those existing elsewhere. The methods outlined in the previous chapter can be used to delineate the effect these factors may have on the demand for transport between cities. We now focus, however, on the aspects of the air transport system that affects the traffic upon it.

Speed is the most appealing aspect of air transport. More precisely, it is not the absolute speed we might reach at some moment, but the overall rapidity of movement from place to place that is important. The capability of traveling hundreds and even thousands of miles in a matter of hours opens up a wide range of opportunities which would not otherwise be available.

The advantages of speed are obtained at a price. The fare for air transport between two cities is generally higher than that of the cheapest substitute. This differential naturally offsets the value of higher speed to a certain extent. Frequently, the tradeoff between extra rapidity and extra cost weighs against the higher speed: it is now certain that practically no one, for instance, would pay the full cost of using the Concorde supersonic aircraft. Hence the decisions of the British and French Governments to subsidize this service. We cannot assume, as many have done in the past, that passengers are automatically attracted to the speed of the aircraft.[2]

Comparison of the prices of tickets does not tell the whole story; we must compare the total cost – and travel time – of traveling door-to-door, from point of departure to point of arrival. To understand why people might choose air transport, we have to look at the whole cost of the trip. Air travel can have a significant advantage in this regard. As compared with going by rail or automobile, it allows one to avoid hotel bills and the cost of meals in restaurants along the way. For business trips of 400 miles or so, such as London to Scotland or San Francisco to Los Angeles, these savings can easily be greater than the extra cost of the air fare. Conversely, the remoteness of an airport and infrequent service to a destination can burden air travel with substantial delays and lead to lower use. Although these costs and delays are peripheral to the air journey, they can have a crucial influence on the level of air traffic.

The configuration of the air transport system largely determines these costs and delays of access to air travel. The location of the airport specifies how long it will take and how much it will cost to reach air transport services. Also, the number and size of the airports in a metropolitan area influence the frequency of service available at each to any destination and, thus, the delays passengers will encounter in waiting for a departure.

The influence of the airport system on the level and distribution of traffic is complicated. This is because its effect is not direct, but indirect by the way the design of the air transport system enhances – or detracts from – the competitive position of an airport with respect to other modes of transport, other local airports, and even airports in other cities.

To clarify these effects, the ensuing discussion focuses on the relationship between the airport and one form of competition at a time, even though they usually appear together. First, we consider a single airport sharing the market with ground transport. We next examine the division of traffic among several airports serving a metropolitan area. Finally, we explore the competition between cities for long distance traffic which might use their airports as an interchange for other destinations. Each of these competitions may alter the traffic at an airport by up to a third.

A. The single airport

The single airport serving a city competes principally with other modes of transport. Its traffic depends on its comparative advantage in providing service. Here, its edge in offering access to rapid transport will be counterbalanced by the potentially higher cost of this service, by the remoteness of the airport, and by the possible lack of frequent departures.

Airports now capture virtually the whole market for long distance trips. The speed of air transport applied over long ranges saves passengers days of travel time, implying substantial economies in meals and lodging while in transit. These days are also valuable: to the person on business for the greater time available for productive work, to the holiday-maker for the extra precious days of vacation. For overseas travel, for example, air transport has virtually eliminated the demand for passenger ships, as Figure 4.1 shows.[3] Much the same can be said for transcontinental travel, although the evidence is less obvious since many people do make the trip by land, some because they find it cheaper but many others because they want to see friends, relatives or sights along the way. In Europe

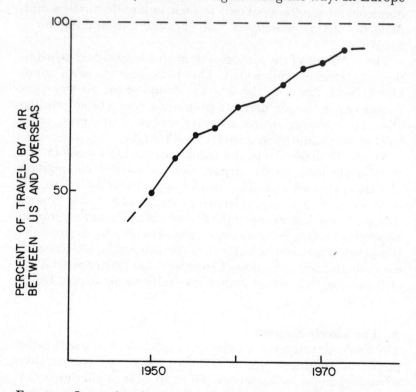

FIG. 4.1   Increasing dominance of air transport for overseas travel

and Japan, the continuing governmental protection and subsidy of the railroads further masks the appeal of air transport.

More and more cargo also goes long distances by air. This traffic is becoming increasingly important for some airports and could at some time conceivably represent a major part of their business. In view of the inefficiency of having airplanes carry dense, bulky materials, however, air cargo will certainly remain a minuscule fraction of the total tonnage sent by rail, truck, and ship.

The airport's share of the passengers going shorter distances is sensitive to the total cost of the air trip. The statistics on travel between Boston and New York, a distance of some 200 miles, illustrate this. In the early 1970s, a combination of events including a massive review by the US Civil Aeronautics Board led to a rise in the basic fare and the removal of family and youth discounts. The resulting increase in effective fares caused air traffic between Boston and New York to drop by about one-third. As shown in Figure 4.2, this effect has persisted, relieved only partially when the scarcity of fuel for automobiles in 1973 encouraged travelers to switch to various modes of public transport.[4]

Any of the various ways airport planners might raise the cost of access to air travel would lead to similar results, in proportion to the amount of increased cost. This would particularly include the construction of expensive facilities, whose costs would be passed on to travelers via higher parking fees, or via eventual fare increases triggered by higher charges for aircraft operations. Consider the case of the passenger terminals at the Tampa Airport: these magnificent structures cost about $6 per passenger in 1973, almost twice the amount typically paid by the airlines elsewhere in the United States. This sum is equivalent to approximately one-fifth of the fare to Miami some 200 miles away. As the airlines cannot absorb extra charges indefinitely, these costs must ultimately be passed on to passengers, and are almost certain to lower traffic noticeably. Any policy to raise taxes or make high profits by taking advantage of the airport's monopoly of landing facilities, as is widely done, can likewise be expected to reduce traffic.[5]

Planning decisions about the location of an airport can significantly affect the difficulty of reaching air services and, thus,

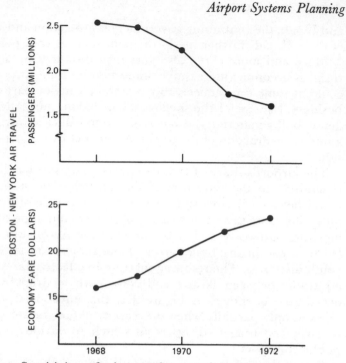

F<small>IG</small>. 4.2   Sensitivity of air travel over short distances to fare
increases

the level of air traffic. This is because there are great pressures
to choose a site far from the city. Modern jets require runways
one to two miles long and force airport developers to seek out
large uninhabited areas. Urban populations also typically want
to keep the noise and pollution of an airport as distant as possible. The result is that the most acceptable sites for new airports
are, from several points of view, far from the center of the city.
The new Montreal/Mirabel airport is some 25 miles from downtown, or some 20 miles further than the old Montreal/Dorval
airport; the Maplin site for the proposed third London airport
was some 35 miles further from London than either of the existing facilities at Heathrow or Gatwick; and so on. Any new airport is almost invariably much further away from town than the
old one. This implies that air services through the new airport
will be relatively less attractive compared to alternative means
of transport, especially for trips over short distances.

Moving airport operations to a new site may reduce short haul traffic by as much as one-third. The case of Detroit illustrates this. In 1947 the city forced all commercial flights to shift their operations to a different airport twenty-five miles further away from the center of the city. This led to an immediate drop in the demand for air transport to cities within 300 miles. As the overall rate of growth in this traffic at Detroit for ten years after the move equaled the rate of growth at all comparable airports in the vicinity, one can presume that this substantial decrease in traffic was also persistent, as Figure 4.3

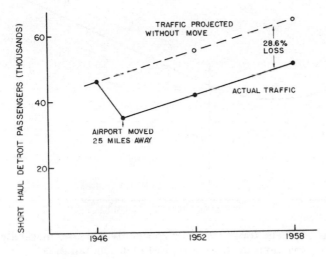

Fig. 4.3 Sensitivity of air travel over short distances to change in accessibility

indicates. We should not, of course, assume that what happened elsewhere, at another time and for a different environment, applies directly to a new situation. But similar drops in traffic are associated with the opening of other remote airports, thus emphasizing the importance of airport location on the level of traffic.[6]

In thinking about the effect of new airport locations, one must be careful to remember that the distance between the airport and the center of the city is only an indicator of the remoteness of the air transport services from potential users. To the extent that many travelers live and work in the suburbs, suburban sites served by good highways are just as accessible overall as locations closer to the city center. Figure 4.4 illustrates this for a hypothetical city: the travel time of the average

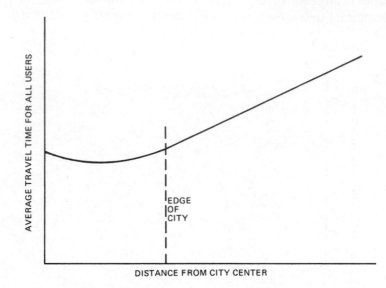

FIG. 4.4   Average travel time to airport only increases markedly for locations far from a typical metropolitan area

user to any point within the city is essentially the same when one takes into account the congestion at the center, and only increases noticeably for sites really into the country. The practical implication of this is that a new suburban airport may be just as accessible, on the average, as one much closer to downtown, and may attract as much traffic. Thus it was in Chicago: the replacement of the close-in Chicago/Midway Airport by the suburban Chicago/O'Hare did not lead to a noticeable drop in traffic.

People wishing to fly short distances have a strong preference for airports that are not far outside the city. The situation at Dallas illustrates this. When all the major airlines moved in 1974 to the new Dallas/Fort Worth Airport, some twenty-one miles from the center of town, the majority of their Texan customers for short flights deserted them, preferring service from Dallas/Love Field right in the suburbs. Southwest Airlines, the only carrier still serving Dallas/Love, thus registered a 40 percent increase in passengers that year. Siting a new airport at a distant location may shift traffic to alternative airports as well as different modes of transport. This bring us to the question of satellite airports.[7]

B. Satellite airports

When airports become congested planners naturally desire to expand their capacity. When this is impossible, the common sense solution is either to build a major new airport as was done at Dallas, or, if this is impossible, to develop some secondary facilities that might handle some of the traffic. Either way, this leads to the situation where one or more satellite airports are associated with the major air terminal for a metropolitan area.

The concept of creating additional airports to accommodate excess traffic is a specific part of the current US national program of airport development. It appears under the heading of 'reliever airports', which, by definition, are 'designed . . . to serve . . . aircraft which otherwise might use and contribute substantially to congestion at air carrier airports'.[8] Unfortunately, as stated in the earlier quote from the UK Civil Aviation Authority and as indicated further below, it does not seem that a policy of building airport capacity is much of a success as far as attracting traffic is concerned. The question is: how will traffic split between primary and satellite airports?

In any metropolitan area where it is a question of creating some relief for congested passenger airports, general aviation and pleasure flights usually operate out of special fields set aside for their use. Hanscom Field is the general aviation airport for Boston, Teterboro for New York, and so on. This activity is thus not central to the question of how traffic will distribute itself between satellites and their principal airports. We most focus on the behavior of airlines and their passengers.

A common view is that the traffic at any airport depends upon

its sphere of influence of 'catchment area'. As the UK Civil
Aviation Authority once put it, the traffic at an airport 'depends
to a large degree on the total number of travellers using it, and
hence on the extent of its catchment area'. The general idea is
that each airport serves a particular territory. This motion is
used frequently in Britain and in the United States. It was the
mainspring of the planning forecast that so wrongly predicted
that Oakland Airport would rapidly take over an increasing
fraction of the air traffic from the San Francisco area as we saw
in the previous chapter.[9]

The expression 'catchment area' indeed conjures up a totally
inaccurate mental image of how people choose transport
services. Rainwater flows down a catchment area to a sewer
according to physical laws; it has no choice as to the direction
it will go. People, on the other hand, do have a choice as to
which airport they use, and differ from water in that they can
and do make a choice. Detailed studies show that people often
deliberately avoid the airport that is closest to them in favor of
a larger, busier facility. Around Cleveland, for example, a
large survey clearly demonstrated that over half of the air
travelers from Akron (a metropolitan area of over 400,000
inhabitants) drive some twenty-five miles beyond their own
airport to obtain service at Cleveland/Hopkins. Examination of
many 'catchment areas' indicates that this is a general rule.
Figure 4.5 shows this using both American and British data.[10]
Satellite airports typically attract only about one-quarter of the
usual number of passengers from their 'catchment area'; the
remainder presumably go to the principal airport.

Frequency of service is often a crucial factor for a person
contemplating which airport to use. The airport with more
flights to a place will almost inevitably offer more convenient
departures. Any resident of an area parking his car at the airport
would also be concerned about frequency of service on the
return: he needs the flexibility provided by backup flights in
case he requires extra – or less – time away from home. Conversely, a person traveling to a city with several airports often
prefers to use the one with the greater service because it offers
more possibilities for transferring to connecting flights. Many
passengers may, of course, attach little or no importance to
frequency. For example, holiday travelers leaving on a charter

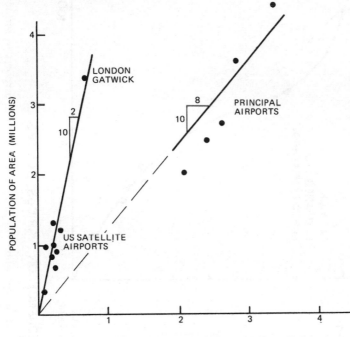

Fig. 4.5 Principal airports attract a far greater share of the market for air travel than satellite airports

flight may only be concerned about a single specific departure. This behavior does not, however, contradict the general rule here, which is that frequency of service is a major factor in determining the attractiveness and use of an airport.

The relationship between frequency of service and its attractiveness is generally represented by S-shaped curves of the type appearing in Figure 4.6. These show how the relative frequency of service between two cities offered by a satellite airport, that is, its frequency share, affects the share of the total market it manages to attract. This phenomenon is also well documented for the competition between airlines on routes linking pairs of airports. The data support the widely held view in the air transport industry that competitors who are able to dominate a market reap substantial rewards and that those who are unable to do so are at a constant disadvantage.

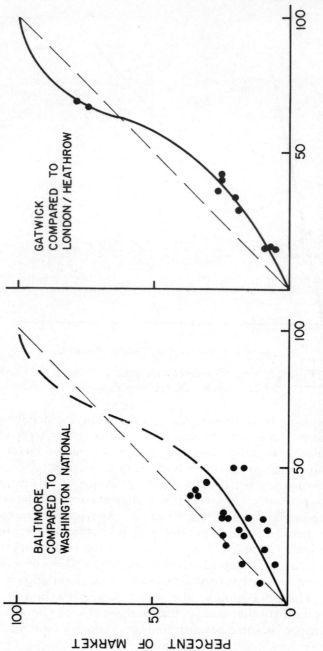

FIG. 4.6 Low frequency service, both on routes and at the whole airport, causes satellite airports to attract lower market shares

Specifically, Figure 4.6 shows that when a satellite airport offers about 30 percent of the flights from a metropolitan area to another city, as London/Gatwick does to Edinburgh, for example, it only obtains 20 percent or less of the market. This implies that the airlines serving the satellite airports will either have to carry fewer passengers per plane or use smaller, less efficient aircraft: either way, this service places them at a substantial economic disadvantage. Furthermore, airlines will find it difficult to overcome this handicap. Even if they increase their service on a particular route from a satellite airport, they will not be able to do anything about the fact that the major airport is inherently more attractive just because it offers more service overall and, thus, more opportunities for connecting flights.[11]

The economic handicap of operating from satellite airports has an obvious message for airlines: they are much better off concentrating their service at the major metropolitan airports. This is exactly what they do, thus leaving the satellites with relatively little traffic. As a rough rule, satellite airports account for only 5–10 percent of the total airline traffic in a metropolitan area.

Absent any regulations forcing airlines to spread their service, competing airports in a metropolitan area only have equivalent levels of traffic when they cater to distinct markets. Thus New York/Kennedy and New York/La Guardia serve a comparable number of passengers, the one on shorter distance, domestic flights, the other on long distance and international traffic. New York/Newark, on the other hand, competes with these airports and manages to attract only a fraction of the traffic they serve, even though it is just as accessible. Its position is rather like that of Oakland with respect to San Francisco. In another vein, Miami and Opa Locka Airports in Florida, Los Angeles International and Long Beach Airports in California, each handle over 400,000 aircraft operations a year, the one handling commercial traffic and the other general aviation and pleasure flights.

These facts have significant implications for airport planning. They emphasize the futility of hoping that airlines will voluntarily spread their service to any great degree over two or more airports in a metropolitan area. Yet sometimes the public interest desires this to happen, either to reduce noise and pollution around a particular part of the city or to secure easier access to air transport for the inhabitants. The evidence then indicates that a policy to distribute traffic to satellite airports will only work if the government pressures the airlines to do this.

Many different kinds of regulations can be used to coerce airlines to serve satellite airports. In the United States, the Federal Government has placed quotas on the total number of operations allowed to use a principal facility. The effect of this policy is uncertain, however. It does encourage airlines to schedule more flights to satellite airports, but there is no control over which destinations will be served from the satellites. Worse, it is almost certain that all the least profitable – and thus least important – flights will be assigned to the secondary airports. This is what happened when the US Government limited the number of airline operations at Washington/National, and forced the airlines to serve more customers from Washington/Baltimore. This quota policy did reduce noise and congestion at the major airport, but did little to enhance the attractiveness of the service at the satellite.[12]

Alternatively, particular airlines can be authorized to operate to only one airport. The British Government, for example, constrains British Caledonian Airways to serve London through Gatwick. This regulation directly helps the policy of developing Gatwick but does impose a substantial economic burden on the airline and weakens – perhaps fatally – its competitive position. These disadvantages could conceivably be righted, however, by further regulations designed to balance the attractiveness of the several airports. A comprehensive policy might thus limit the frequency of service from London/Heathrow and Gatwick and other destinations, or institute differential fares between these points. As of late 1975, the British Government finally recognized this problem and authorized a £2 (about 10 percent) discount on fares from London/Gatwick to Scotland for the explicit purpose of counterbalancing the inherent advantages of London/Heathrow as the larger airport.

Second airports can also be developed by forcing airlines to carry out specific services at designated sites. This procedure is aimed precisely toward the desired objectives, but can be circumvented. The attempt of the US Federal Aviation

Administration to develop Washington/Dulles by requiring all long distance traffic to use that facility has not really worked: domestic airlines continue to use Washington/National by transforming long haul flights to short haul flights through stops at Chicago, Atlanta or other closer points. The result is that, in 1973 for example, only one-sixth as many passengers used Washington/Dulles as Washington/National. The British Government somewhat more successfully encouraged the development of London/Gatwick by transferring all British flights destined for West Africa and much of South America to that location. But passengers do not have to fly British or even travel through London. London/Gatwick still only accounts for a small fraction of the traffic through the London airports.

The French effort to develop the new Paris/de Gaulle Airport in combination with Paris/Orly was more drastic. It was successful to the extent that it did channel comparable levels of traffic through both locations. But it was unfortunate in that it noticeably decreased the quality of air services through Paris and thus seems to have reduced traffic, and in that it imposed high new expenses on the airlines. The French reasoned that Paris was a metropolitan area of nearly 10 million inhabitants, that many cities of 5 million or less had substantial airports, and therefore that it was reasonable to split Parisian air services into two halves.[13] This they did by fiat. The airlines who had to split their services were then immediately saddled with the extra cost of duplicate staff and of transporting crews between airports; Air France alone reportedly spent $2·5 million on this account in the first year. Travelers also found that connecting flights were much less convenient from either airport, now that frequencies were roughly halved, and began to bypass Paris by making connections through other cities.

Planning for second airports is, indeed, not just a question of organizing the competition between airports in a metropolitan area. It also requires that we think through the services provided by our airports to the entire air transport network, and the competition offered in this regard by airports in other cities.

C. Airports and the air net
Airports are not just local facilities, they are part of the entire air transport network. They potentially serve a much wider

market than the metropolitan area in which they are located. In addition to handling the traffic originating in and destined for their immediate region, they function as transfer points for passengers and goods coming from and going to distant cities. This transfer traffic faces different alternatives, as it traverses the air net, than the local traffic, which is tied to a specific area. The transfer traffic can often be routed through other points and is, thus, susceptible to the competition offered by other airports on the air net.

Transfer traffic can be very large. At Atlanta transferring passengers outnumber those originating in the city by almost three to one. At many other major airports they account for approximately half of all the passengers boarding the aircraft. Even at smaller airports handling three to four million passengers a year, transfers may represent 20 percent of the total. Whatever planning decisions do to influence the attractiveness of an airport to transfers may change the total loads on the facility.

Transfer traffic is also volatile. Having no intrinsic reason to pass through any particular point, it can – and often does – appear and disappear rapidly. Its patterns are sensitive to the wide range of elements that constitute the environment for air transport. Political changes can be crucial. The independence of the Portugese colonies, for example, reduces the need to reach them via Lisbon and thus lowers air traffic through that city. Similarly, easier East-West relations could divert the flow of air traffic between Europe and Asia from the Middle East to the USSR, thus diminishing traffic at Bahrein, Teheran, and other stopover points. Aeronautical developments can be equally important. The introduction of modern, long range jets has completely reshaped the pattern of transfers across the world. Just as Gander and Shannon are no longer necessary stops across the North Atlantic, Denver is no longer a major stop for transcontinental traffic across the United States.

Here again, however, frequency of service is a fundamental consideration. Frequent departures increase a traveler's chances of making an easy connection to another flight, and minimize the possibility that he will have to wait a long time for transport to his destination. This is the phenomenon that Parisian airport authorities failed to recognize fully in planning for the new

Paris/de Gaulle Airport: by reducing the service available, they drastically diminished the attractiveness of Paris as a transfer point and undercut its share of the market.

To plan airport systems properly, we must try to anticipate the fluctuations in transfer traffic. This means that we must understand the basic forces that shape the development and evolution of the air transport network. We must, in particular, see what influences airlines to change frequency of service at airports.

A transport network always represents a compromise between two major goals: the desire for short, direct connections between any two points, and the desire for frequent service. If airlines scheduled direct, non-stop services between every point, many would necessarily either be very infrequent (would Manchester-Geneva or Syracuse-Nashville rate more than a couple of flights a week using modern airliners?), or would be much more expensive if smaller aircraft, with higher costs per passenger, were used. Although direct services are convenient if a flight happens to be leaving when you want it to, they also imply low frequencies, correspondingly long waits, as well as higher costs. To overcome these difficulties, airlines encourage travelers from smaller communities to proceed to their ultimate destinations via larger hub airports. These detours obviously increase the time some passengers spend flying, but there are compensating advantages. By concentrating their traffic, the airlines have more passengers on fewer links, can provide more frequent service and may also be able to use larger, more economical aircraft, and thus can reduce the overall cost and time of many trips.

At some point the possible savings in time and money due to concentration of airline service equal the extra cost and travel time inherent in more indirect or circuitous travel. This trade-off is mediated, however, by the fact that many travelers are actually not sensitive to frequency of service. These forces determine the basic shape of the air transport net and, consequently, the intensity of transfers at the hub airports. Finding the best pattern of service is an arduous process, since even a small number of airports imply an enormous number of distinct possibilities; fortunately, recent computer-based methods simplify the problem considerably.[14]

Technological and demographic changes can shift the balance between the advantages of concentration of traffic and the disadvantages of circuitous travel. They thereby also alter the percent of transfers. Anything that raises the overall volume of traffic, for example, makes it economical to offer more frequent service on direct flights and, thus, reduces the motivation for concentration and decreases transfers. The introduction of larger aircraft, on the other hand, makes many direct flights unprofitable, increases the concentration of traffic and, therefore, raises the traffic at hub airports while decreasing the number of flights at smaller airports.

The effect of the introduction of larger aircraft on traffic can be dramatic. When jets came into use in the early 1960s, replacing smaller turbo-prop and propeller aircraft, many smaller cities lost almost half their air service – in a period of rapidly growing demands for air service in the country as a whole! Figure 4.7 illustrates this sudden drop. As the chairman of the US Civil Aeronautics Board put it 'The local service carriers

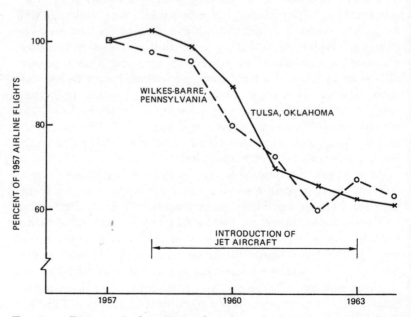

FIG. 4.7   Decrease in frequency of service accompanies the introduction of larger aircraft

have been transformed ... Their smallest aircraft are at least double the size of (those) they began with ... (They) have focused their energies on the ... higher density markets. The result has been that service to smaller communities has become less.'[15]

Much the same result occurred in the early 1970s along with the introduction of widebody aircraft. As figure 4.8 indicates,

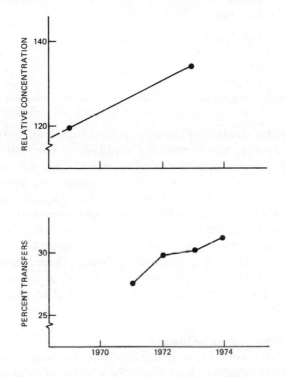

Fig. 4.8 Rise in transfer rates at hub airports accompanies decrease in connectivity of network

both the concentration on the air transport network and the percent of transfers at major airports increased during this period. The traffic at the major transfer points correspondingly grew about twice as fast as traffic elsewhere, as Table 4.1 shows.

These observations emphasize that planning for any airport

TABLE 4.1   *Passenger traffic grew faster at airports with higher percent of transfers during the introduction of jumbo jets*

Airport Type	Location	Percent Transfer Traffic (*1974*)	Annual Percent Traffic Growth (*1971–1974*)
Transfer	Atlanta	73	13
	Dallas	55	10
	Chicago	47	7
Low Transfer or Terminal	Los Angeles	22	4
	San Francisco	21	5
	Detroit	15	5
	Boston	10	4

must consider the role of the airport in the air transport system and, specifically, the potentially rapid shifts in traffic due to competition from airports in other cities. This has not been done systematically in the past. Yet the continued failure to do so could prove terribly expensive in terms of wasted resources. As a recent study of the problem put it 'old methods of forecasting either national totals or individual airport traffic independent of service patterns will produce many mistakes in airport planning ... It is our fear that, using these methods of forecasting, excess capacity will be created in many smaller airports and too little capacity will be added at existing hub cities ...'[16]

D. Planning implications

The fact that airports exist in a competitive environment underscores the idea that we should plan for systems of airports rather than individual airports alone. As the preceding discussion indicates, the traffic at any location depends significantly upon the development of services by other modes of transport and by other airports, both locally and further afield. Any planning process which fails to take this into account will, almost inevitably, find that its plans are inappropriate if not wasteful. We need to develop airport planning on a national or at least a regional scale.

In this connection we should recognize that the development

of a realistic process for planning airport systems will be difficult. As indicated in Chapter 2, there is widespread reluctance – especially in the United States – to accept effective planning of a whole system. The industry has yet to acknowledge fully the costs of an individualistic, myopic view which neglects the behavior of the system.

The evidence also emphasizes that the behavior of the air transport system is, indeed, highly complex. As of yet, only a few tools exist for examining the full interaction of the demand for services with their supply, or even the interaction of different airports. The S-shaped curves provide a picture of the performance of satellite airports, and some new computer-based methods of analysis suggest how traffic flows across the air transport network could be analyzed. These approaches are still crude, however. This means that considerable research is needed on the behavior of transport networks.

Finally, we should be fully aware that the future performance of the air transport system is inherently uncertain. Quite apart from our own ignorance about how the system works, the detailed distribution of traffic between airports is highly volatile. These facts reinforce the recommendation, introduced in Chapter 3, that airport planning must be flexible in its approach to problems and formulation of solutions.

5   Getting There and Back

It is, of course, necessary to provide adequate access between any airport and the region it serves. This is usually done by building short connections between the airport and the metropolitan highway network. Passengers, employees and delivery vehicles can then get to and from the airport using any of the broad array of automotive means of transport available in the area: cars, buses, taxis, trucks, and so on.

Reliance on the automobile is a simple way to provide access. It may even be highly profitable! With any luck at all, the airport can expect a sizeable income from parking lots. Both in the United States and Britain, the airport authorities typically obtain about 15–20 percent of their income from parking.[1] The relative importance of parking revenues naturally depends upon local administrative arrangements. The different national attitudes toward public subsidy or exploitation of air transport similarly distort financial comparisons.[2] But it is still clear that parking lots can be good business. The standard method of providing access to the airport therefore has much to recommend it to airport authorities.

A. High-speed mania

For some time, however, airport planners have been dissatisfied by the automobile as a means of providing airport access. They are frustrated by the fact that constant improvements in the speed of air travel have not been matched by comparable developments on the ground. They have been especially aggrieved since the introduction of jet aircraft, which almost halved the flight time between many points. For flights of less than 600 miles, which carry most of the air passengers in Europe, the United States and elsewhere, it is now commonplace for the trip to and from the airport to take as long as the trip in the air. This is what is commonly known as the 'airport access problem'. Something, the reasoning goes, must be done to 'right the balance' by reducing travel time to the airport.

Airport planners have consequently been anxious to build special facilities to transport passengers to and from airports. Their basic objective is to avoid the congestion and delays that occur on metropolitan highways at peak hours. The obvious solution is to establish a separate route to the airport, that excludes other traffic, and is designed to permit high-speed travel at all times. Practically every major airport has seriously considered some proposal for high speed access. And almost all proposals have been variations on this theme.

Any system of high-speed access to an airport would be very expensive. Several proposals would cost over $300 million each – as much as one-third of the cost of a completely new airport. Few of the proposals even claim that these high-speed systems would cover their expenses, let alone be as profitable as the parking garages they would supplant.

Is the emphasis on high-speed access to the airport really appropriate? What problems would these systems solve? Are these investments an effective way to improve air transport? What should we in fact do to help people and goods get to the airport? Before attempting to answer these questions, let us look more closely at some typical proposals for high-speed access to airports.

One approach is to build a motorway or limited-access highway just for the users at the airport. This was done for Dulles Airport in Washington and for the Dallas/Fort Worth Airport. Of course, these expressways only provide rapid access if there is no congestion. To make this approach work, the designers have to provide substantial overcapacity that, in turn, leads to high cost per user. At Dallas/Fort Worth, for example, it costs $0·25 just to drive on the Airport's internal roadway. The greatest disadvantage of the private highway, however, is that it can only serve its purpose for the distance one can build a motorway into the city. Generally, this is not very far. The Dulles access highway is useful for only one-third of the way into Washington, until it meets a circumferential highway that can be extremely congested. Because special airport motorways are only feasible for a limited distance, they cannot provide the kind of access planners have wanted.

Proposals for high-speed access to airports have thus focused on various types of railroads. The great advantage of this approach is that it is fairly easy to find a path for a railroad into the center of the city, either along existing tracks or via a tunnel. But these proposals are expensive, For example:

(1) New York has planned to implement railroad services from Manhattan to Kennedy and Newark Airports. Even though these two systems would use existing tracks for most of the way, they would cost over $400 million each.

(2) Montreal proposed to inaugurate a railroad, capable of cruising at 100 miles an hour between the center of the city and the new Mirabel airport, some thirty-five miles away. The cost was estimated at $438 million in 1973.

In addition, Munich, San Francisco, Chicago, Philadelphia, and other cities are actively considering building or extending rapid transit lines to serve their airports. The cost in each case would be around $100 million or so.

The predilection of French and American planners for sophisticated solutions, discussed in Chapter 2, is evident here also. Both countries have generated highly technocratic variants of the railroad proposals. Indeed,

(1) The Aéroport de Paris for many years pushed for the construction of a 125 miles-per-hour aerotrain between its two major airports, Orly and de Gaulle.

(2) The US Department of Transportation for a long time advocated a similar concept, the tracked air cushion vehicle, to link new airports at Los Angeles and Miami with the existing sites.

These alternatives differ from the more conventional railroad approaches only in that they would be faster, more expensive and presumably more experimental and less reliable.

Other possibilities for bypassing congestion deserve mention. First there is the concept of off-airport terminals which would receive passengers or cargo shipments and place them on some sort of collective transport. The general idea is to organize many individual trips into a few larger movements, thereby reducing congestion and increasing accessibility. Use of public transport also reduces costs to the passengers, but at the inconvenience – often overwhelming – of requiring them to detour to the off-airport terminal and to wait for a departure to the airport. To service many customers at a satellite terminal, some kind of special building or bus station is required, such as the former British European Airways terminal in West London or the East Side Airlines terminal in New York. Shifting patterns of population, rising labor costs, and the increased availability of the automobile tend to make such investments uneconomical and, indeed, led to the demise of the facilities mentioned. If only a few passengers are to be served, a schedule of limousines or coaches can be operated from existing bus stations or hotels at minimal costs. Such services operate efficiently from the New York airports to the suburbs and at most major American airports. These systems are self-supporting as a rule, but typically only carry 3–5 percent of the airline passengers.

Alternatively, helicopter or some sort of air service is frequently advocated as a rapid means to bypass congested access on the ground. This high-speed service is possible but turns out to be uneconomical. All existing systems of this sort require extensive subsidies, costing about $10 per person roughly, to attract passengers away from the (sometimes) congested facilities on the ground.

B. The airport access problem

All these proposals to solve the 'airport access problem' are implicitly based on a common understanding of what the facts are and of how society ought to react to them. The validity of the solutions naturally hinges on whether these perceptions are correct. So we ought to consider carefully whether the model of the problem realistically represents the actual situation.

The developers' usual model of the airport access problem has three main elements:

(1) First, it supposes that many people want to go between the airport and the center of the city or at most a few locations. Hence the plans for railroads with few – if any – stops between the city and the airport. This is what is proposed for New York. Similarly, the British Airports Authority

originally advocated a direct railroad line between Heathrow and Victoria Station in central London.

(2) Second, the model assumes that air travelers value their time highly. It then concludes, since airports are quite far from the city, that customers will insist on rapid access to the airport. Hence the emphasis on making it possible for them to move through the city at 100 miles an hour and more, speed unavailable to others in the metropolitan area.

(3) Finally, the model presumes that the presence of congestion on the way to the airport requires the development of special facilities for the airport traffic. Naturally, these delays occur at the peak hours of traffic when everyone else is trying to get to work or go home. The model thus implies that a minority of air travelers should get better service than a majority of commuters.

Is this model reasonable? To what extent do the public agree with the facts? Is much of the airport traffic really destined to the center of the city? Are air travelers prepared to pay for extra speed on the way to the airport? Would a high-speed facility, that requires people to go to a special terminal and wait for a departure, actually save them any time? And there is also the ethical issue: is it right for air travelers to receive preferential treatment?

The answer to each of these questions is generally no. The model of the 'airport access problem' is basically deficient. Except in rare cases, the proposals for high-speed access to the airport do not represent a good investment: they do not provide enough service to justify the cost. The traditional means of getting to and from the airport – automotive transport of some kind – is almost universally more economical for society. Let us see why.

C. Nature of access travel

Many people travel to and from an airport. On a typical day, over 100,000 trips are made in and out of the larger airports in Paris, London, New York, Chicago, and Los Angeles. Superficially, this represents an obvious opportunity for mass transport. But the number of people who travel between the airport and the center of the city is really quite small, as can be seen by looking closely at who travels to the airport.

It should first be pointed out that only a fraction of the passengers using an airport travel between the airport and the city or region it serves: many transit from one flight to another and never leave the airport. As Table 5.1 shows, as few as

TABLE 5.1   *Percent of passengers using access facilities in major United States cities (domestic, interstate travelers in 1974)*

City	Percent	City	Percent
New York	94	New Orleans	76
Boston	90	Cleveland	75
Detroit	85	Minneapolis–St. Paul	74
Philadelphia	85	Kansas City	72
Houston	83	Honolulu	69
Tampa	82	St. Louis	62
Las Vegas	82	Pittsburgh	59
Seattle	80	Denver	54
San Francisco	79	Chicago	53
Washington DC	78	Dallas/Fort Worth	45
Los Angeles	78	Atlanta	27

one-third (at Atlanta) and commonly only four-fifths of the passengers use the access facilities.[3] This observation also means that discussing any requirements for access facilities as a ratio of the number of passengers must be somewhat suspect. Nevertheless, since this is the practice of the industry and since the ratios are imprecise in any case, the ensuing discussion follows custom in this regard.

Who then travels to the airport? The precise answer differs for each airport and varies from year to year, but a representative estimate can be made.[4] Although crude, it is satisfactory as a general guide to the situation.

(1) One-third of all access trips are made by employees working at the airport or on the airlines. The number of workers is frequently about 1·5 per 1,000 passengers per year, but varies considerably according to the kinds of activities at the airport. The ratio is only about 0·3 employees per 1,000 passengers at New York/La Guardia, which serves a heavy

commuter traffic, but as high as 3 per 1,000 at Miami, where important maintenance bases are located. For practical purposes each worker makes a trip to and from the airport about 250 days a year. All together, employees generate about 0·75 trips per passenger.

(2) Only about one-third of all access trips are actually made by air travelers. Persons using an airport count as different passengers for each flight, and many merely transfer from flight to flight instead of coming to or going from the airport. Air travelers thus account for less than one, and generally around 0·75 access trips per passenger.

(3) The remainder of the trips, one-third or somewhat less, are made by delivery vans, sales representatives, service vehicles, as well as visitors of all sorts.

This information indicates fairly obviously that relatively few people travel between the airport and the center of the city. Few employees will pay the high prices for housing in the city; they tend to live in the suburbs. Service vehicles and the like may pick up some cargo downtown, but many are oriented toward industrial areas closer to the airport. And even most passengers disperse to homes and offices throughout the metropolitan area. Only a fraction of them go to hotels and offices in the center of the city. In San Francisco, for example, merely 20 percent of all passengers go to the central city. Higher figures which are quoted are often misleading. While over 40 percent of all New York passengers are said to go to Manhattan (that is just half of the travelers leaving the airports), this covers an area of about twenty square miles. The fraction going to any specific central point is no more than a tenth, at most.

The net result is that the volume of traffic between the airport and the city center – or any other point – is quite low. For airports serving 10 million passengers a year, such as Paris or Boston, we can expect only about 10,000 persons a day to travel between the airport and the downtown area. The number might rise to 30,000 daily for the largest airports such as Chicago/O'Hare. But since the capacity of a modern railroad or subway can easily reach 30,000 persons per hour in each direction, the airport is a rather limited market for any airport railroad. So much for the first assumption about the airport access problem.

What about the second assumption? How highly do air passengers value their time? How much are they prepared to spend for faster service to the airport? Airport planners frequently presume that airports serve the important businessmen who will pay considerably to save time on the trip to the airport. To what extent is this true?

Many passengers are, in fact, on business and may not be paying the costs themselves. They are all also richer than the average: in the United States their salaries may easily exceed $20,000 a year, implying hourly wages of over $10 an hour, or far more than the typical American worker. Finally, the cost of their transportation is substantially greater than it would be if they went by rail or bus. These observations emphasize that some air travelers could pay a significant premium for faster service to the airport. But would they in fact? What do they really choose to do?

All else being equal, travelers are certainly sensitive to the time it takes to get to the airport, especially for short flights. Whenever this time suddenly increases, local air travel drops sharply. This happens, for example, when a new airport far from the city opens to replace one closer to town, as occurred recently for Kansas City and Houston and earlier for Detroit, as discussed in Chapter 4.

The fact that air travelers can be sensitive to time does not necessarily mean that they would pay substantially to reduce the travel time to the airport. The persons who stopped going by air when the new airport in Detroit opened found that the move made air travel inherently less attractive: they switched to rail, bus or car, because these modes of transport offered a better combination of price and travel time. Passengers are sensitive to costs also, and they would have found air travel less attractive even if the longer trip to the more distant airport were replaced by a faster, but more expensive, journey. To explain their behavior we cannot focus on only one dimension of the service, such as speed; we must consider all the important factors for the entire trip.

Considering the entire trip, it seems unlikely that most people who pay a substantial premium to travel by air would pay very much for faster access to the airport. The special value of air travel lies in the major opportunities it opens, not in the minutes it saves. Business travelers making a short trip, say from London to Glasgow or from Boston to Washington, value air transport because it saves them a whole day of travel: at the very least this represents a savings of overnight accommodation and means that going by air may actually reduce the cost of the trip! A faster trip on the ground does not translate into any obvious monetary savings; it may mean more time to work – or to while away. Similarly, vacationers value air travel because of the special holidays it permits. They do not demand high-speed access to the airport. Quite the contrary: the majority of them prefer to accept the considerable delays of charter flights in order to save money.

Most air travelers in fact plan to spend considerable time at the airport. Even in the United States, where passengers can commonly board flights right up to the last moment, about half of them arrive at the airport an hour or more before their scheduled departure. They may easily come two hours earlier for international flights which require customs checks, or when airlines refuse to board passengers who arrive close to the departure time, as they do in Europe (see Figure 5.1). Naturally, there are exceptions: experienced commuters boarding shuttle flights, as between Boston and New York or London and

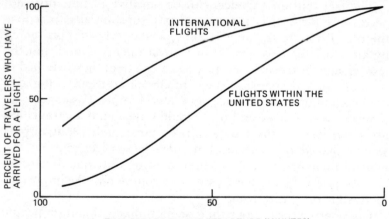

FIG. 5.1   People typically arrive early at the airport and wait there a considerable time

Glasgow, may arrive with only a few minutes to spare. But many people are generally uncertain about where to go and anxious not to miss their flight. Experienced flyers also often choose to arrive early; once their business is over in a city, they might as well wait at the airport as anywhere else. So the usual pattern is that many travelers plan to wait at the airport.

For most people, the value of time spent waiting is low. Many air travelers will consequently not want to pay much for extra speed on the trip to the airport. Indeed, available evidence on how people respond to changes in fare and speed on the access trip, indicates that passengers are about twice as sensitive to the cost of this trip as to its speed.[5]

As regards the third assumption, that the existence of congestion requires that society do something about it, we must recognize that this is not so. Something should be done only if the possible results justify the effort. The data so far imply that the economic justification for high-speed access to airports is weak, and indeed it is almost always lacking. Are there other viable reasons: does social justice or the national interest require such investments? It would appear not. The important officials or others for whom the government wants express service can be provided for by helicopters or other means. Vacationers and others are not likely candidates for subsidies. As air travelers are furthermore generally more affluent than the rest of the population, the notion of favoring them with special grants is offensive to general views of social justice.

A close examination of the nature of travel to the airport indicates that the plans for high-speed systems for airport access are based on false hopes. A large market for travel between the airport to the center city does not exist. These few passengers are not prepared to pay significantly for speed. It appears wrong to give them this service as a present. High-speed systems therefore seem inappropriate. But what should be done to promote access between the airport and the region it serves?

D. Effective solutions

Transport to the airport can be provided in many ways: automobiles, taxis, microbuses or limousines, buses operating on the public highway or on lanes reserved for their own use, helicopters, and so on. In general, a variety of means should be used to serve the needs of different kinds of passengers: the visitors going to hotels in the city, local residents coming from the suburbs, a few travelers in a great hurry, and others who are less demanding. But not all possibilities should be implemented. Some are fast, but too expensive; others are inexpensive, but too slow or inconvenient to have wide appeal. An attractive middle ground exists between these extremes.

Which forms of transport are most desirable depends upon local circumstances. Public transport is more appropriate for cities with high densities of population, like London or New York, than for spread cities like Los Angeles or Denver. It is also more appealing when the airport is relatively far from the city. Similarly, rail transport appears more attractive when the service to the airport is only a marginal extension to a system of mass transport for commuters and other urban travelers. No solution is, therefore, best for all circumstances. But it is nonetheless practical to determine which possibilities are more likely to be desirable.

The alternatives which provide the best blend of economy and speed can be found by what is known as a cost-effectiveness analysis. The procedure is simple in principle and generally useful for a wide variety of problems. As it does require many calculations, however, it is most easily carried out using a computer of some sort. The analysis first computes the cost of providing some levels of service (or effectiveness) of any system. For airport access this means determining the total cost and travel time for a trip to or from the airport by each of the alternatives worth considering. These results identify the system which provides the best service for any given cost. This is a cost-effective solution. For different levels of costs, different designs, providing better or worse service according to whether we spend more or less, are cost-effective. In practice, a particular system is usually best for a range of costs. The set of the best or most cost-effective solutions thus consists of a few different systems. Which of these is preferable depends on how much one is prepared to spend for better service, in our case, for faster access.[6]

A valid comparison of different forms of transport requires that we examine their service over the entire trip, from the first start – at the home or office, say – to the final destination at the airport. This is a basic principle. It is no good simply to contrast the average speeds of a train and a car, for example. Travelers are not interested in such abstract motions; they want to know what it takes to complete the entire journey. Analysts find it easy to forget this principle, especially since it requires considerable effort to estimate the total cost and travel time of any trip. But it is absolutely essential to remember, if we wish to understand what kinds of transport are most effective in providing service.

The trip taken on public transport takes longer and costs more than would appear from the published schedules and fares. It includes not only the obvious cost and delay of the trip on the system itself, but also the time and cost of the trip to the railroad or bus station, the wait for the departure, and the transfer from the terminal to the final destination. These additional costs and delays can easily be as large as the costs and travel time by public transport. Under these circumstances a great many people will be much better off taking a car, their own or a taxi, to or from the airport.

If public transport has its own right-of-way, it does have a significant advantage over automobiles: it can avoid traffic jams. This is important for commuters who move during the rush hours. But it is not significant for most air travelers: strange as it may seem, only a few of them travel at the rush hour. Studies have repeatedly shown that the congestion in airport access at the rush hour is predominantly caused by airport and airline employees; they may then constitute up to 80 percent of the airport traffic.[7] Public transport can thus be expected to be less effective for airport access than for urban transport generally.

This discussion puts the conclusions of the cost-effectiveness analysis into perspective. Figure 5.2 shows typical results. These concern a hypothetical medium airport with about 5 million passengers a year, in a city with densities typical of urban areas in Europe or the East Coast of the United States, with the airport five miles from the center. A situation rather like Philadelphia, Copenhagen, or Hong Kong, for example. Similar results, with somewhat different costs but with the same policy implications, obtain for the broad range of possible situations.[8]

Automobile systems almost universally provide better service

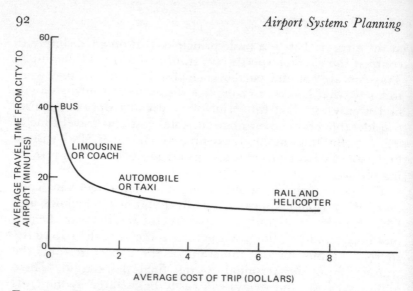

Fig. 5.2 Typical results of the evaluation of various alternatives for access from city to airport

at less cost for airport access. Travelers find personal vehicles most attractive and use them if available. Otherwise, they prefer taxis, airport buses, rental cars and the like. The principal advantage of automotive systems is their flexibility, their ability to pick up and distribute people near where they are or want to be. These systems are also relatively fast, except at the rush hour which is important only for relatively few air travelers; and inexpensive, since the cost of the vehicles can be spread over so many other kinds of trips.

Rail and rapid transit systems are generally cost-ineffective for airport access: they provide too little service for the cost. If many people were prepared to spend $10–$15 to save half an hour of travel, these solutions might cover their costs. Since most people do not value their time so highly, especially when going to the airport, rail solutions require extensive subsidies except in rare circumstances. This is clearly the case for the existing installations at Brussels, Cleveland, Tokyo, and Paris/ Orly, which fail to cover their operating costs, let alone to repay their cost of construction.

Although rail systems are not economically justifiable for airport use alone, it may be appropriate to link the airport with a comprehensive network of urban mass transport. Under these circumstances, rail access to the airport may be viable. Insofar as it would then be able to distribute persons all around the metropolitan area, it would appeal to employees and others at the airport who would not be interested in a special service to the center of the city. And the average costs per passenger of the system would be further reduced to the extent that it would be used by commuters and other persons moving about the city. The connection from Heathrow Airport in London to the underground railway thus makes much more sense than the special rail service to Victoria Station that had been originally planned. Much the same can be said for the proposed rail service from Montreal to the new Mirabel Airport. Its justification is that it would really be a commuter railroad and not a special airport service: four-fifths of its traffic would be commuters and the like, only one-fifth would have anything to do with the airport.[9]

Alternatively, rail access may be justified as a spur to a national network of rail transport, as for Frankfurt-am-Main and possibly for Paris/de Gaulle and the new airport for Munich. Where an off-shore airport must be connected to the mainland, as for a new airport in Osaka Bay, rail service might save considerably on the cost of constructing tunnels. Generally speaking, however, any system which requires travelers to go to a station and wait for a departure is likely to provide worse service, at higher cost, than automobile solutions. The exceptions are for airports which process many passengers oriented toward the central areas, and have congested road links and easy access to rail service. This is London/Gatwick, truly a rare example.

Proposals for satellite terminals, designed to process passengers or cargo at locations away from the airport, are unlikely to succeed as a general rule. The effort and cost involved in making the detour via the off-airport terminal, plus the cost of the building itself, are generally not worth any savings achieved. An exception occurs when substantial traffic is concentrated around a particular point and the airport is relatively far or difficult to reach, thus increasing the advantages of collective transport. Off-airport terminals for passengers have thus been successful, on a small scale and for a few years, in London and

New York, for example. Satellite facilities also operate successfully for low volumes which can be processed incidentally through airline offices or hotel lobbies. Limousine and coach services operate successfully on that basis in North America and various other cities such as Athens, Zagreb, and so on. An off-airport terminal for air cargo has operated profitably in New York's Garment District, but, because of the extremely high cost of handling cargo at any point, facilities for consolidating cargo shipments are usually not worthwhile.[10]

Analysis confirms what we might have suspected: the fancy technocratic approaches providing access to the airport are not economical. They offer little extra service, for a few people, at great expense. But economics is not everything, of course. Society may choose, for a variety of reasons, to limit the use of automobiles and to favor and subsidize public transport. This by itself is not, however, a sufficient justification of rail access to airports. The money spent on serving 10,000 air travelers a day could just as well serve 100,000 or more commuters a day, as can be seen by comparing the plans for the Kennedy Airport Access Project in New York with parallel projects to extend railroad service to residential areas. A decision to favor special systems for airport access implies a judgment that air travelers deserve preferential treatment. But as they are richer than most people, this is an argument for a subsidy from the poor to the rich, a position difficult to sustain overtly in a democratic society. Economically and ethically, it seems that the usual automotive solutions, using either private car or public bus, provide the most desirable means of handling the kind of highly dispersed traffic that flows to and from the airport.

E. Coping with the automobile

Automotive traffic at the airport requires three kinds of facilities: highway lanes, both to the airport and inside it to serve internal traffic; curb space at which to pick up and deliver passengers; and parking space for the storage of vehicles. The need for them greatly depends upon local practices, especially the fraction of the passengers who transfer at an airport and thus do not use the access facilities. It can also be changed by various strategies for controlling traffic. But some general guidelines may be useful.

One should anticipate that approximately as many vehicles come to the airport as passengers who board aircraft. In the United States the ratio is around 1·3 vehicles per passenger, and comparable levels of traffic exist elsewhere. This figure is so high not because of the vehicles used by the passengers directly but because of the cars used by employees, the delivery vans, service vehicles, and so on. At a major airport in which the peaks of traffic are not too severe, about 0·3 percent of the total annual traffic occurs each day, and about 1/3000th during the busiest hours. For an airport of ten million passengers a year, such as Boston or Frankfurt-am-Main, about 4,000 vehicles per hour reach the airport during peak periods. They require three lanes of traffic each way, especially allowing for some growth. (At London/Heathrow, one of the busiest airports in the world, there are only two lanes each way through the tunnel to the passenger terminals. While cargo vehicles use another route, it is easy to see why the tunnel presents a problem.)

The amount of curb space needed for loading and unloading passengers can be very large. It is often an important constraint on the design of a terminal.[11] In the United States, designers typically allow 4 inches per 1,000 passengers in a year; for London/Heathrow the ratio is closer to 3 inches. For an airport of 10 million passengers a year, this amounts to about half a mile. As one is naturally reluctant to build terminals so long, this requirement encourages the design of terminals with redundant facilities, for example: with two levels, one for arrivals and one for departures; multiple lanes for automobile access, as in Chicago; or underground or nearby parking facilities providing easy access.

The requirement for curb space is sensitive to the amount of time drivers can loiter. Relatively little space is needed in London, where vehicles can only wait two and a half minutes on the average. Elsewhere, where traffic is not regulated strictly, it may be necessary to provide up to twice as much space. A design for the new terminal at Maiquetia in Caracas allowed for close to 8 inches per 1,000 passengers a year, for example. This standard implies a lot of expensive construction. It is often much cheaper to solve the problem by hiring policemen to control traffic.

Space permitting, the larger American airports provide about

125 parking spaces per million passengers a year, and about 500
spaces per 1,000 employees. In all, this works out to about 500
spaces per million passengers. In the United States the ratio
ranges from as low as 300 for crowded airports, to as high as
1,000 or more for smaller terminals. In Europe the figure is
generally closer to 300, as might be expected with lower levels
of car ownership. London allows for 50 spaces per million
passengers plus 240 per 1,000 employees.[12] A great deal of
parking space is needed anywhere.

The requirements for parking space can be limited if necessary – as it is within the tightly constricted terminal areas at
Heathrow and Los Angeles. The demands for space depend on
how long people park their cars, a factor that is sensitive to the
prices charged for parking. They can be drastically reduced by
selectively discouraging the few people who park their cars for
several days or even weeks. Typically, about three-quarters of
the parkers stay less than three hours, using about a fifth of the
total space; only about 10 percent stay over twelve hours, but
they use about three-quarters of the total space provided.
Higher rates on long-term parking can easily discourage
travelers on extended trips from leaving their cars. Employees,
who can account for well over half the total parking space on
the airport, can similarly be stimulated to use remote lots, as at
Heathrow or Kennedy in New York. These actions can significantly reduce the demand for valuable expensive space close
to the terminals. Of course, since the operation of parking
facilities can be so profitable, this policy may only be desirable
when lack of space compels it.

All in all, it is difficult in the abstract to establish in advance
what the details of an access program for any specific airport
should be. Experience elsewhere only suggests guidelines that
have to be refined by detailed local surveys and analysis. The
basic facts of the matter are sufficient, however, to recommend
an overall strategy. This policy is to rely on automobile transport, private or collective, as the least expensive means to
provide access to the airport for most people, recognizing that
rare exceptions to this rule can be justified in truly exceptional
cases.

6 Designing the Terminal

The airport terminal provides the connection between the aircraft and the vehicles for ground transport. This function is difficult to perform well: the different size and length of stay of the air and ground vehicles imply quite dissimilar amounts of space on the airside and landside of the terminal. Typically, the stands for stationing the aircraft must occupy a much longer distance than the curb needed for the loading and unloading of cars, buses or other such vehicles. How to balance these conflicting requirements on opposite sides of the same building, is the essential question of terminal design. Until recently, this may not have been either a major or an important problem. Things are different now.

Terminals and related facilities for serving passengers used to account for only one-quarter or less of the cost of an airport. Until about 1965 or so, most of the money had to be spent on making runways and taxiways longer, wider and stronger to accommodate new generations of aircraft, especially the jets. This has changed. Aircraft manufacturers now recognize that airport designers find it nearly impossible to extend their runways, or to obtain space near cities for airports with runways over two miles long. They have consequently designed the latest generation of aircraft, the 747 jumbo jets, the widebody aircraft and the airbuses, to operate on existing runways. But these new aircraft, serving hundreds of passengers at a time, require much larger terminal facilities than were needed before. Most of the money for airports, about three-quarters or so in the United States, will now be spent on terminals.

Individual terminals can be extraordinarily expensive. Construction costs of $100 per square foot are commonplace both in North America and Europe. The American Airlines building in Boston cost close to $60 million when opened in 1975. Including the value of the money invested, amortization and maintenance, this amounts to between $5 and $10 per passenger for the life of the structure. The Pan American Terminal at New York/Kennedy reputedly cost over $140 million. An airline could go broke on terminals alone!

These costs emphasize that terminals should be designed with the utmost care. Lack of forethought can – and frequently has – cost millions. Unfortunately, airport planners have tended to think simplistically about the design of terminals. We have a long way to go before we will really know (rather than think we know) what solutions are best for particular problems. Meanwhile, we can hope to understand the forces that shape this decision, and to decide which concepts of design are most effective for different situations.

In trying to understand how to design terminals, we should recognize the limitations on our ability to define the best solutions. Terminals simultaneously facilitate a wide range of services for many users: arriving passengers, transfers, commuters without bags, travelers with many, visitors, and so on. There is no clear way to determine the cost of each service, let alone how greater expense will improve service by itself. Essentially the same persons at the same counters check baggage and tickets and perform other functions, for example; on what basis could we arguably specify the cost of carrying out either service, or project how that service alone would improve if we increased the available staff and equipment? On logical grounds, any kind of cost-effectiveness argument concerning services that are performed simultaneously is likely to be dubious. Clear guidelines for specifying in detail the best levels of service for a terminal may thus be unobtainable.

A. Available concepts

Airport planners generally agree that the designs for terminals can be placed into three categories. The code-words used to describe each type differ from place to place but, once personal preferences for names are set aside, consensus exists about the possibilities.[1] Using descriptive terms, the concepts for terminals are

(1) centralized, with either finger piers or satellite subterminals linking passengers and aircraft;

(2) linear or 'gate-arrival', in which aircraft are all parked close to the access highways; and

(3) open-apron or 'transporter', using a bus or special vehicle
to carry passengers between the terminal and the aircraft.

As experienced travelers know, each airport terminal is
unique in any number of respects. With few exceptions each of
them can, however, be fitted into this typology. The categories
represent fundamentally different visions of how a terminal
should function and whom it should serve.

The characteristic feature of a centralized terminal is a common hall through which passengers pass. This central area
contains the facilities for checking passengers and for handling
their bags, and also houses the auxiliary services such as restaurants and stores. Passengers connect with the aircraft by going
along corridors. If the positions for the aircraft are located
along the corridors, we have finger piers. If they are placed at
the end of corridors, we have satellite terminals. Figure 6.1
shows examples of both types. Except that satellites may allow
somewhat more room for aircraft to maneuver, depending on
their location, they provide essentially the same services as
finger piers. If the airport is very large, the terminal area may
include several centralized terminals. This occurs at Paris/
Orly, London/Heathrow, Chicago/O'Hare and San Francisco,
for example.

Centralized terminals have many advantages. Airlines and
airport operators like them because they promote intensive use
of facilities and equipment and thus reduce the average costs
of providing check-in and baggage-handling services. Passengers who have to transfer between flights also tend to like
centralized terminals because they are relatively compact.
Customs and security officials appreciate the fact that they can
control passengers with only a few checkpoints. Centralized
terminals also facilitate access to public transport, particularly
rail, as found at London/Gatwick and Frankfurt-am-Main.

Conversely, the essential disadvantages of centralized terminals is that – at large airports – they force passengers to go
through a confusing, busy place and to face some considerable
distance between the vehicles that bring them to the airport and
the aircraft. The example of this that is always cited is Chicago/
O'Hare, where the greatest distance from aircraft to a parked
car is close to half-a-mile; but this implicit comparison with

other terminals is unfair because Chicago/O'Hare is by far the busiest airport – other designs would have equivalent problems if they had to operate at the same scale. This distance to the aircraft gate may be covered on foot or via some form of moving sidewalk or automatic device like the 'skybus' horizontal

CENTRALIZED
WITH
FINGER PIERS

FRANKFURT/MAIN

CHICAGO/O'HARE

CENTRALIZED
WITH
SATELLITES

PARIS/DE GAULLE
(COMMON TERMINAL)

TAMPA

LINEAR OR
GATE-ARRIVAL

DALLAS/FORT WORTH

KANSAS CITY

TRANSPORTER

WASHINGTON/DULLES

FIG. 6.1   Examples of use of pure concepts for terminal design

elevators in use at Tampa or Seattle/Tacoma. It can in any case be an inconvenience, especially to commuters and others who may be in a great hurry.

The gate-arrival concept was devised to eliminate long distances between arrivals and the aircraft. The intent is to allow a passenger to be driven right up to the aircraft stand, that is, right up to the gate between the terminal and the aircraft. With this scheme, the airport is spread out linearly, with roads on one side and aircraft on the other, as Figure 6.1 illustrates. The concept of airports completely designed around gate-arrival terminals became fashionable in the late 1960s, possibly because few people had experienced, or thought deeply about, the disadvantages of this approach.

The implementation of a gate-arrival terminal naturally requires separate baggage-handling and check-in facilities at or near each aircraft position, significantly increasing the number and cost of the equipment and staff needed to serve passengers. Also, because the terminal is laid out in a line, the maximum distance from one end to the other is much longer than it would be for a centralized terminal of comparable size, especially if the gate-arrival terminal has aircraft on only one side of the building. The gate-arrival terminal can thus be quite unattractive both for transferring passengers and for returning travelers who wish to pick up cars they may have parked in front of some distant gate.

The third concept substitutes vehicles for most of the terminal structures. These vehicles, generically called either transporters or 'passenger transfer vehicles', carry passengers between a central terminal and the aircraft parked on the apron.[2] This is sometimes called the open-apron concept because most buildings have been removed. The prototype for this arrangement is Washington/Dulles which uses transporters to serve essentially all passengers (a few walk to small aircraft through a minuscule finger pier).

As far as the passenger is concerned, the transporter terminal functions very much like any centralized terminal equipped with devices to reduce walking. One difference is that, if all passengers must use the transporters, none of them can get to the aircraft as rapidly as they might be able to in a design with finger piers. For airlines and airport operators this concept is potentially expensive since it requires a large labor force of drivers and attendants. It is also potentially economical, since transporters can be parked: vehicles have to be operated only when needed and drivers can be hired for a fraction of the time, either for a specified shift or season. The transporter concept thus has a distinct economical advantage for handling peaks of traffic.

B. Simplistic practice

Each of the available concepts of terminal design functions efficiently for some kinds of traffic. Centralized terminals are easier for transferring passengers, customs control and access to public transport; gate-arrival terminals are better for commuters; and transporter designs handle peaks of traffic more economically. As any airport is likely to have a significant proportion of more than one of these types of traffic, we should expect that effective designs for terminals would deliberately combine the available concepts.

Industry practice has, however, been simplistic in its choice of concepts. Airport designers have typically developed their master plans for terminals around only one of the three available concepts. So far, this rule seems to have only a couple of exceptions: the British Airports Authority has been innovative in its use of transporters around London, and of gate-arrival terminals in Scotland, and a few other airport authorities have also adopted hybrid designs of some sort. The general situation has been that planners argue, often bitterly, about which concept is best for all purposes.

This debate has been remarkably dogmatic. Recent controversies over new airports have demonstrated a singular unwillingness to compromise or to combine design concepts. The protracted arguments over the new Mirabel Airport for Montreal illustrate this. The architects and planners in charge decided early on that a transporter design should be built, and resisted compromise when airlines and others subsequently showed them that this plan had several drawbacks. Finally some sort of combination of concepts was agreed upon, but only after various airlines applied strenuous pressure. Elsewhere, for example at Frankfurt-am-Main, Dallas/Fort Worth and Washington/Dulles, the situation was similar: politically powerful institutions or persons imposed their favorite design on the users.

This controversy seems totally unnecessary. From a logical point of view it is obvious that a diversity of needs may be best served by a mixture of the elements that best serve each need. We should start with the premise that the best design for an airport terminal is likely to be a hybrid of the pure concepts.

Yet a rational combination of elements is difficult to achieve in practice. Why is this so? What are the forces which put us into this position? If we could understand this, we could perhaps resolve the problem.

One answer to this question is that most airport designers have been trained to seek elegance of design. In the United States, the persons who design airport terminals are mostly architects. They naturally think of form and external beauty. In France and Germany, the airport designers are engineers who, in accord with their kind of technical training, tend to like mathematically clever and geometrically pure designs.

In any event, the aerial views of the plans for practically all new airport terminals are remarkable for their symmetry, elegance, and even beauty. This can be seen by looking at Dallas/Fort Worth, Paris/de Gaulle (illustrated in Figure 6.1) as well as Berlin/Tegel, Cologne and San Francisco. From a bird's-eye view, there is no question that the plans are a success. But few people ever really see or appreciate this. Geometric symmetry of the exterior shell is an abstraction prized mainly by designers; it is rarely even noticed by others, who are too busy trying to find their way around.

The users and operators of an airport terminal mostly want the system to function smoothly and efficiently. They want a variety of distinct services, such as easy access to all aircraft and easy transfers, that call for different forms to fulfill these functions. The diversity and complexity of their pragmatic desires inherently clash with aesthetic preferences for simplicity of concept and form.

This reasoning implies that we can develop better terminals for the airlines and the travelers if we concentrate our attention on the functions to be served, not the form. We may need to restrain the architectural considerations to the extent they inordinately dominate the design process.[3] Instead, we need to emphasize pragmatic, economic considerations in the selection of the concept for the terminal. These are largely missing. The problem is to determine what combinations of concepts provide the most suitable design for the particular mix of traffic at any airport. To do this, we need to understand the different kinds of traffic using airport terminals, and their implications for the choice of design.

C. Nature of the traffic

To understand a problem, we have to measure its important characteristics. Here is where we often fail: we readily assume that the statistics available are suitable for our purposes. This is not necessarily so. The appropriate description of a situation depends upon our point of view. A professor looking at a classroom will count the number of seats, for example, while the junkman will estimate the pounds of scrap. Conversely, statistics developed for one purpose are not generally useful for other purposes. Knowledge of the quantity of scrap in a classroom does not help the professor plan her seating arrangement.

Various organizations collect extensive data about air travelers at any airport. Customs officials count the international passengers; air traffic controllers the aircraft movements; airlines the passengers and their destinations, and so on. These groups do not gather statistics for the benefit of terminal designers. They collect the data for their own administrative purposes and may be quite willing to accept peculiarities that are inappropriate for designers. Air traffic controllers, for example, count training flights together with actual airline arrivals. This practice makes sense in terms of keeping track of their work load, but is confusing to the designer interested in the number of aircraft that need to be accommodated at the terminal.[4] In designing terminals, we must thus first of all be most careful in interpreting data about airport traffic.

Where data are concerned, airport planners focus on the problem of identifying the daily and hourly volumes of future passengers and aircraft which the facilities should accommodate. As described further in Chapter 7, the object is to obtain reasonable approximations to the peak flows so that the elements of the terminal can be sized correctly. These figures are useful for calculating the capacity of the system for handling bags, the width of the corridors and other dimensions.

The data available in current practice is almost useless for helping planners decide what kind of terminals to build. They offer few clues as to whether gate-arrival or centralized terminals are better, or how they should be combined at any airport. In providing data that tell how wide to build a corridor, they say nothing about what function that corridor should perform or how it should relate to other parts of the terminal. The effort directed toward sizing elements of the terminals begs the more fundamental questions: how should these elements be combined and what should the overall terminal look like? Unfortunately, current practice does not routinely generate the information necessary to address these basic issues.

What information would be most helpful in deciding upon the right mix of concepts for a terminal? Which aspects of the traffic have the most important consequences for its performance? The answer is that we should focus on data that relates directly to the choice of terminals. Since major functional differences between the alternative design concepts lie in their ability to handle transfers and to deal with peaks of traffic, we should closely examine the variations in the level of traffic and the percentage of traffic. Conversely, the conventional categories of traffic used in terminal design – for example, the number of passengers on business or pleasure, or the number of male or female passengers – do not tell us very much about what combination of concepts are right to use for a terminal. One usual series, data on international traffic, can be helpful. For many airports, such as Boston, these figures help define the highly peaked daily and seasonal traffic across the Atlantic. International traffic also favors the use of centralized terminals that facilitate immigration controls.

The relative importance of transfers at an airport is a significant factor for helping decide among concepts for terminal design. It is also most difficult to determine. No agency regularly collects data on the number of passengers transferring between flights. These statistics must be pieced together indirectly or measured by sample survey.[5] Table 6.1 shows some typical results.

The percentage of transfers varies greatly. Some airports,

TABLE 6.1   *Percent of passengers transferring between flights at major United States Cities (domestic, interstate travelers in 1974)*

City	Percent	City	Percent
Atlanta	73	Los Angeles	22
Dallas/Fort Worth	55	Washington, DC	22
Chicago	47	San Francisco	21
Denver	46	Seattle	20
Pittsburgh	41	Las Vegas	18
St. Louis	38	Tampa	18
Honolulu	31	Houston	17
Kansas City	28	Philadelphia	15
Minneapolis–St. Paul	26	Detroit	15
Cleveland	25	Boston	10
New Orleans	24	New York	6

such as Atlanta, Dallas/Fort Worth and Chicago/O'Hare function as major interchanges. It therefore stands to reason that their terminals should emphasize convenient accessibility between all sections. (From this perspective, the gate-arrival design implemented at the new Dallas/Fort Worth Airport would seem to be the wrong kind of solution for this location, since it impedes transfers between terminals. It is interesting in this connection to note that American Airlines has made Dallas/Fort Worth into a major interchange point for its own passengers, confident perhaps that few of them will now be able to switch easily to a competitor at a different terminal.)

The importance of transfers is also difficult to determine because the persons going from one flight to another represent only a fraction of the people effectively transferring. This is especially true at decentralized terminals. Indeed, many passengers may park their cars near one section of the terminal, from which they depart, and then return, on a different airline or from a different city, to another section. To get back to their car, they must go through the terminal area just as if they were transferring. We may call these people crypto-transfers; 'transfers' because they move through the terminal like transfers, and 'crypto' because they are hidden from ordinary observation. The problems of these travelers may actually be the worse of all: they have to handle their own bags, while a passenger connecting between flights can rely on the airlines to do that chore.

These additional transfers may be important at some airports. While no direct measure exists for these crypto-transfers, circumstantial evidence suggests that they can be numerous. After the opening of the gate-arrival terminal at Kansas City, for example, it was noticed that many passengers avoided the parking lots near the gates, and preferred the more distant – but centrally located – spaces. This effect was certainly reinforced by the fact that the central parking was cheaper. Nonetheless, the same effect appears to occur at Dallas/Fort Worth. As a guess, that requires further verification, crypto-transfers may account for as much as 10 percent of the traffic through the terminals.

The variability of the flows of traffic is another major determinant of the choice of terminal concepts. When the traffic fluctuates widely, many of the facilities needed during peak periods will be idle much of the time. Under these circumstances, it becomes economical to turn off their cost when they are not required. This cannot be done with buildings, for which most of the cost is fixed in the structure. But it can be done with transporters, for which most of the cost lies in the operating expenses of the drivers, fuel, and maintenance. Transporters can be parked when not needed, and drivers can be hired only for a specified shift or season. The transporter concept is most economical for handling peaks of traffic.

Some representative monthly variations in traffic appear in Figure 6.2. This graph shows the number of months for which the passenger traffic exceeds any given percentage of the month with the least traffic. The steeper the slope, the greater the peaks in the traffic.[6] Typically, smaller airports serving vacation resorts, like Grand Junction, Colorado, or Ibiza, Spain, have the greater seasonal variations. Larger tourist attractions, like Mexico City or Miami, may have substantial peaks around the weekends, when holidays usually begin and end.

For New York, the strongest peaks occur in the international traffic. For a brief two months (the July and August vacations period) about half again as many passengers require service as at any other time during the year. Similar vacations occur around

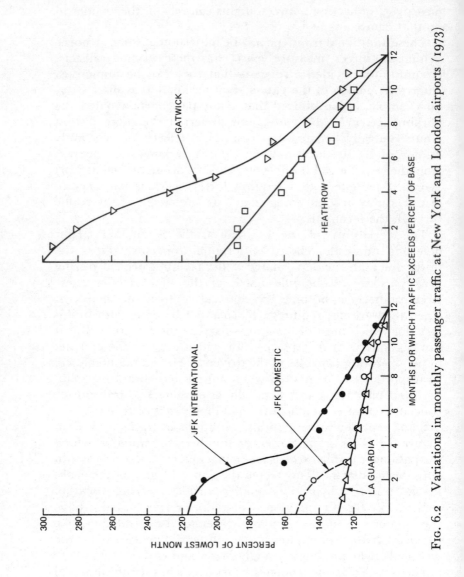

FIG. 6.2 Variations in monthly passenger traffic at New York and London airports (1973)

London. But notice that there the major international airport, Heathrow, has a fairly even pattern of traffic. International traffic, which is inherently seasonal in much of North America, is otherwise in Europe. What happens is that the holiday traffic, which gets routed through New York/Kennedy, goes through London/Gatwick or Luton via charters (or 'non-scheduled' carriers, as they are often called in the United States). The wide variation in holiday traffic is emphasized by Zurich, which publishes separate figures for scheduled airline service and charters, as Figure 6.3 shows.

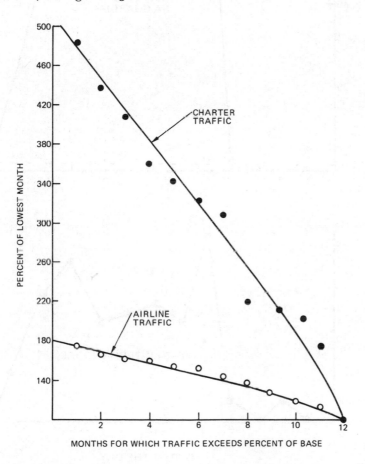

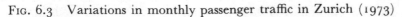

MONTHS FOR WHICH TRAFFIC EXCEEDS PERCENT OF BASE

FIG. 6.3   Variations in monthly passenger traffic in Zurich (1973)

Daily fluctuations can also be important. Some airports, such as New York/La Guardia, are steadily busy through most of the day while others, like Miami, evidence sharp peaks, as Figure 6.4 shows. Some airports are also sensitive to particular

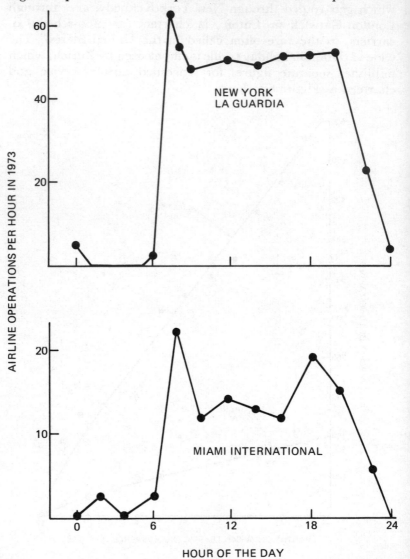

FIG. 6.4   Examples of different kinds of daily fluctuations in traffic

travel patterns or to time zones.[7] New York/Kennedy for example, is particularly busy from two in the afternoon, when the mid-day flights arrive from Europe, until nine at night, when these aircraft depart. At other times the airport is virtually deserted. The pattern of international traffic through Montreal has a similar peak, and this provides a strong justification for the use of transporters at their new Mirabel International Airport. Conversely, such peaks argue against the trend to construct large terminals dedicated to international traffic at North American cities such as Boston and Chicago. This conclusion, however, runs counter to most city pride.

Lack of punctuality of the arrivals of aircraft also influences the utilization of facilities and, thus, the desirability of transporters. A large proportion of the flights routinely fail to arrive on time, through any of a variety of meterological, mechanical, and other problems. Equipment and staff have to be available for serving the aircraft much longer than is needed to perform the operations. The resulting relatively low levels of utilization of fixed facilities favors the use of transporters.

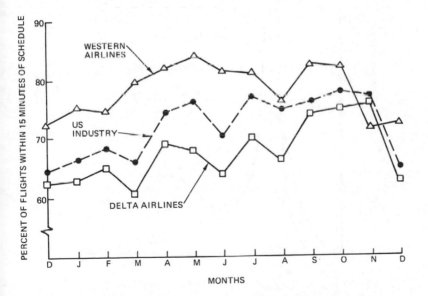

FIG. 6.5   Variation in punctuality of aircraft arrivals and departures in the United States (1973)

Flights are not particularly punctual. Defining being on-time as operating within fifteen minutes of schedule, which is the generous definition used by the United States airlines, nearly one-third of all flights are not on-time as Figure 6.5 shows. To a certain extent, punctuality depends upon the climate and deteriorates during both the winter, when bad weather causes delays, rerouting and cancellations, and during seasonal storms such as the August tornados and thunderstorms in the United States. But it is also a matter of airline policy. Some airlines deliberately hold back flights so that connections can be conveniently made from other flights which happens to be late. This is especially true of Delta, for example, that consistently has a lower percent of its flights on time.

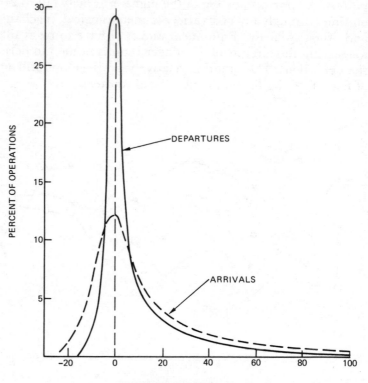

FIG. 6.6   Typical variations in punctuality for arrivals and departures of aircraft

In detail, the arrivals and departures of aircraft typically deviate considerably from their schedules. Figure 6.6 shows that many flights are more than twenty minutes late, with arrivals spread out over more time than departures.[8] It should be emphasized that, as Chapter 4 indicates, the patterns of transfers and peaks vary over time. As air traffic develops in a region and more direct flights become available, the number of transfers at some airports may decrease significantly. Or they may increase. The introduction of aircraft with transcontinental ranges eliminated many of the stops and transfers that used to occur in Denver, but they also created Copenhagen's position as a gateway to transpolar flights from Europe to Western United States.

The intensity of peaks in traffic can also change noticeably.

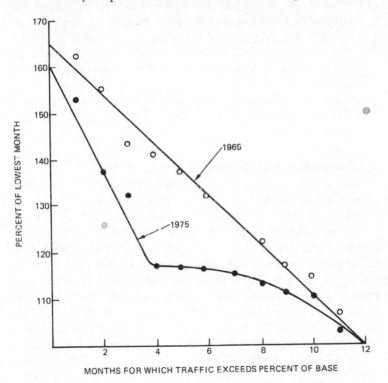

FIG. 6.7 Variation in peaks of passenger traffic at Los Angeles International

They can increase for airports that develop greater vacation traffic, and can decrease strongly for airports like Los Angeles that become more routine or business-like destinations, as Figure 6.7 suggests. Punctuality of aircraft may also vary as the facilities for air navigation and maintenance improve, and as an airport becomes congested and delays build up. No firm rules on these trends can be established. We simply need to remain flexible, to design our terminals so that they can accommodate various levels of traffic, spread in different ways across the days and years.

With these data in mind, let us examine the major questions concerning the fundamental nature of terminals at an airport. These are:

(1) Should the facilities be centralized in a single major complex? Or decentralized into separate terminals or gates as with the gate-arrival concept?

(2) Should transporters be used exclusively, as at Washington/ Dulles? Partially, as at many European airports? Or not at all?

(3) To what extent should the facilities be shared by different airlines, as they are in Europe and generally not in the United States?

D. Centralized or decentralized?

A centralized terminal facilitates transfers. It generally implies smaller distances for persons connecting between flights. This is not to say, of course, that the distances are necessarily short: end to end at Chicago/O'Hare is over a mile. Large as this is, it is less than the comparable figure for a gate-arrival terminal: the greatest distance between gates at Dallas/Fort Worth, an airport with less traffic, is more like two miles. A central terminal makes it possible to keep transfer passengers within a single building and thus reduce the number of stations needed for security inspections. It also provides an easy connection to a mass transit system. The railroad station for the Frankfurt-am-Main Airport is right below the central terminal building and curb, for example. But at an airport with decentralized terminals, such as New York/Kennedy, it is essentially impossible to locate stations which would be convenient to each unit.

A central terminal also creates congestion. This is both good and bad. It is good because it creates the density of traffic needed to support restaurants, shops and other passenger conveniences. Only minimal coffee shops survive at gate-arrival terminals, where this density does not exist: nobody can afford to maintain the equipment and staff required to provide full food service just for the few persons who pass through a couple of gates. Conversely, however, the congestion at centralized terminals can delay and confuse traffic, and is exactly the kind of inconvenience gate-arrival terminals are designed to overcome. Qualitatively, gate-arrival terminals are most convenient for commuting passengers going frequently to the same destination: they have little concern for transfers or for special shops and services, and probably want to proceed as quickly as possible to their flight.

From an economic point of view, the question of which configuration is better depends on the tradeoff between the extra costs of providing more facilities with more staff at decentralized terminals, and the savings that occur by avoiding the delays and confusion that occurs in a centralized terminal. The extra cost of operating a gate-arrival facility can be quite high. This design requires separate check-in counters for every few gates, and prevents staff from being used for many flights at once. Braniff and TWA each estimated, for example, that they needed 15 percent more staff to serve their new gate-arrival facilities at Kansas City.

The complexity and cost of the equipment required to sort bags and cargo in a large terminal is the most powerful economic incentive for decentralization. Complicated mechanisms may have to be provided to sort this traffic through the confusion of a central hall serving dozens of destinations. Strong diseconomies of scale exist in this process: costs increase exponentially faster than the size of the terminal. Specifically, a recent study estimated that, for cargo facilities

$$\text{Total Costs} = \text{Constant} \times (\text{Area})^{1.16}$$

Although this exponent appears small, it can have important implications: it says that buildings ten times the size cost almost 50 percent more per unit area! This disadvantage of large size exists even in the presence of significant economies of scale in the construction of buildings, thus emphasizing the tremendous cost of sorting packages, as Figure 6.8 shows.[9] Trading off the extra costs of gate-arrival terminals and the diseconomies of sorting processes in a central facility one finds that gate-arrival terminals are marginally less expensive for many large cargo operations.

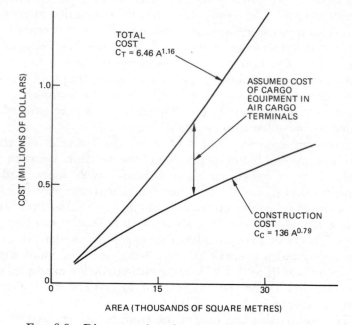

FIG. 6.8   Diseconomies of scale in cargo terminals

The situation is less clear for passenger terminals. Whether, or when, diseconomies of scale exist for these facilities is not known. But because passengers try to find their own way and require only minimal assistance, it is almost certain that the diseconomies of scale will be less for passenger facilities than for cargo terminals. This means that gate-arrival terminals probably lose a marginal economic advantage, and that central terminals may be less expensive for passengers.

A hybrid terminal may be best for many situations. To meet the conflicting desires of different passengers for ease of access and of transfer, and to keep costs within bounds, it may be most effective to include both the centralized and gate-arrival concepts in an overall design for a terminal. The gate-arrival section can serve heavy commuter traffic to a few destinations, and the finger piers the remainder of the passengers. In practice, this is the formula that has successfully evolved at New York/La Guardia, where the shuttle passengers to Boston and Washington have their own gates. A similar design is planned for the

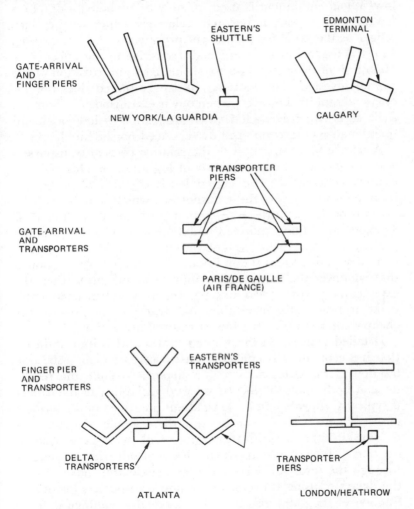

FIG. 6.9 Examples of use of hybrid concepts for terminal design

new terminal at Calgary, where, as Figure 6.9 shows, the gate-arrival facilities will serve the commuter traffic to the provincial capital at Edmonton.

E. What about transporters?

Transporters become more economical than constructed gates when the rate of utilization for the facilities becomes relatively low. When equipment is used for only a few hours a day or a few months a year, it becomes relatively expensive per passenger as the same fixed costs get prorated over fewer people. Constructed facilities are especially sensitive to this effect since almost all of their costs consist of the fixed amortization of the capital invested. The cost per passenger served does not increase so rapidly, however, when one uses transporters. Some of their costs can be avoided when utilization is low: fuel and maintenance costs drop, and drivers need not be hired.

A schematic comparison of the relative costs of transporters and of constructed gates appears in Figure 6.10. This graph is entirely conceptual. The actual levels of the curves depend both upon the costs of the transporters, which may be as little as $50,000 for a fairly ordinary airport bus to as much as $400,000 for a fully equipped mobile lounge that can raise the passenger compartment; and on the cost of the structures, which is most sensitive to local conditions. The crucial observation is that whatever the relative costs may be at full utilization, the exponentially rising cost per passenger of constructed gates make it practically inevitable that transporters provide the cheaper alternative at the lowest rates of utilization.

Detailed analyses in the United States and Britain indicate that it is economically efficient to use transporters for a sizeable fraction of the gates at a major airport.[10] While the results depend both upon the local costs and variability of the traffic, it typically appears best to serve about one-third of the aircraft positions with transporters. Because these should be gates with the lowest rates of utilization, they will only serve a small fraction – about 10 percent or less – of all the passengers through the terminal. Relatively few would thus have to face the delays of using transporters. Using transporters for only a fraction of the gates also has the practical advantage that an airport is not as vulnerable to a drivers' strike as it could be if transporters were the only means of connecting passengers to aircraft.

The economics of transporters are sensitive to anything that influences the relative costs of capital. High interest rates make transporters more attractive, for example. But high inflation, which increases the cost of salaries and fuel and reduces the real cost of construction, favors constructed facilities.

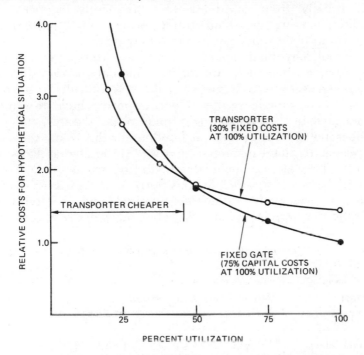

FIG. 6.10   The relative costs of fixed and mobile gates depend upon the utilization

Transporters are particularly attractive in special circumstances which make constructed facilities especially expensive or impossible to obtain. United Airlines recently estimated, for example, that transporters are desirable whenever the costs of constructed facilities exceed $3 million per gate. They are also useful when lack of space prevents immediate expansion, as has been the case at Atlanta. Because transporters can be acquired rapidly, they can also provide service to growth in traffic which occurs before constructed facilities are ready, as they have done at Toronto and New York/Kennedy.

Traffic patterns which lead to low rates of utilization of equipment also favor transporters. They are thus especially advantageous for situations where there are significant peaks in traffic, either daily or seasonal. Likewise, they are relatively economical for airports at which flights typically deviate substantially from schedule. This frequently happens at facilities serving long-haul traffic, where small percentage changes in flight time translate into long delays.

Overall, a hybrid design including transporters is particularly appropriate when there are marked fluctuations in traffic, or when expansion of constructed facilities is difficult. Table 6.2 shows some examples of this. The transporters have proven to be effective in accommodating summer peaks of traffic, and are deliberately part of the plan at London/Heathrow and the new passenger terminal in preparation for Air France at Paris/de Gaulle. They also economically provide for rush hour traffic on a daily basis and are used for this purpose at Paris/Orly-West, which is principally a domestic terminal, and at Montreal/Mirabel. The original plan at Mirabel, incidentally, was to use

TABLE 6.2   *Examples of existing and planned hybrid designs for airport terminals*

Concepts Blended	Terminals which are Hybrid In Fact	By Design
Finger Pier/ Transporter	Atlanta (Eastern and Delta use some transporters)	London/Heathrow Paris/Orly-West London/Gatwick
Gate-Arrival/ Transporter	Montreal (Air Canada, others will use gate-arrival)	Paris/de Gaulle (Air France Terminal)
Finger Pier/ Gate-Arrival	New York/La Guardia (Eastern's Shuttle terminals function as gate-arrivals)	Edinburgh/Glasgow Calgary (Edmonton Commuter Service will be gate-arrival)

transporters exclusively, but the Canadian domestic airlines appear to have persuaded the authorities to permit some aircraft to dock directly at the terminal.

F. Shared use or not?

The size and cost of terminals can be reduced by arrangements to share their use among several airlines. This practice is commonplace in Europe and essentially everywhere except the United States: an airport authority typically operates the gates and other ground services for the benefit of everyone. Similar procedures for the non-exclusive use of gates by airlines exist in the United States at Honolulu and for various international terminals, such as the International Arrivals Building at New York/Kennedy. Many airlines in the United States also reportedly contract with other airlines to share the use of gates otherwise used exclusively by a single airline.

The advantage of shared use is that it allows more flights to be squeezed into any given number of gates. By cooperating, airlines can make use of facilities that would otherwise be idle due to scheduled or random variations in traffic. This advantage is counterbalanced to some extent, however, by the difficulty of maintaining coordination between airlines, the expense of making equipment compatible and by the airlines' sensitivity to loss of image in competitive markets.

As indicated previously, the inevitable deviations from schedule force planners to provide more facilities than necessary if all went well. When a flight does not leave on time an extra position may have to be provided to accommodate an arrival. Overall, this phenomenon may necessitate easily half again as many gates as would be needed if aircraft actually were able to perform on schedule. In practice, this number is estimated through a detailed examination of the activities anticipated at an airport.

The essential features of the phenomenon are captured in the following approximate formula:

$$\text{Gates Required} = (\text{Gates needed by schedule}) + (\text{Gates needed by schedule})^{1/2}$$

This is crude but does emphasize that the extra slack that must be made available decreases, as a fraction of the total, for larger

airlines or operating units. For example, if the schedule called
for nine gates, six more would be specified by formula, leading
to a 9/15 or 60 percent utilization at peak periods on the
average; if the schedule of a larger airline called for sixteen
gates, the formula would call for a 67 percent utilization at the
peaks. This is illustrated in practice by operations at San
Francisco shown in Figure 6.11: the largest airline felt it could
plan its activities around a 70 percent utilization at peak
periods; the next largest apparently only dared go as far as a
60 percent rate.[11]

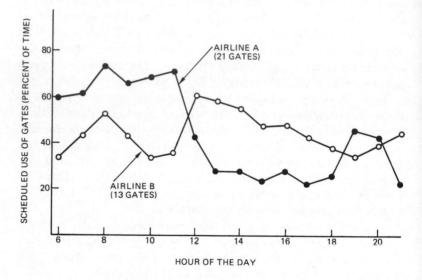

FIG. 6.11   Scheduled utilization rate for gates at San Francisco
(1971)

Considerable savings can thus result from the combination of
several small operations into one common service for all. For
example, if four airlines each have a scheduled need for five
gates each, they would require about 80 percent extra if acting
separately, but only about 45 percent if acting together. A
total saving of 35 percent would theoretically be possible for
that case. Only relatively small savings might exist if we combine large operations. Joint use between two airlines requiring
forty gates each would lead to only a 10 percent reduction in

facilities, an advantage which could easily be eliminated by other factors.

Further savings can be achieved through shared use when the airlines serve markets whose traffic peaks at different times. This effect depends upon the degree of overlap between their needs. Figure 6.11 indicates how demands of two major airlines can complement each other: at San Francisco the airline serving the eastern United States features many early departures to make for reasonable times of arrival in New York and elsewhere, whereas the airline going north-south needs the most gates after noon. To give some idea of what can be done, the Aéroport de Paris found that effective sharing by airlines with different traffic patterns reduced the need for gates at Orly-West by about 15 percent.

The major argument against some amount of joint use of facilities is not one of fact, since it is generally agreed that this approach can be economical, but one of principle. Airlines that compete against each other feel that they must be visible if they are to be successful. This implies that they want their own facilities. In many places, this argument has less force because the airlines are tied together by the so-called pooling agreements, according to which they pool their revenues and share them according to predetermined formulae. Despite this pooling

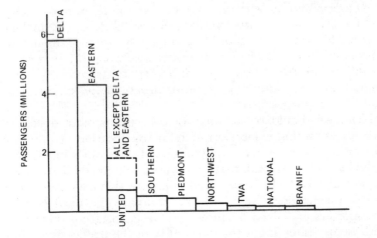

Fig. 6.12 Passengers processed by each airline at Atlanta (FY 1974)

agreement, and perhaps because they are renegotiated from time to time, airlines serving major routes outside North America do often vigorously maintain their identity, as British Airways and Air France have done by serving Paris from different terminals at London/Heathrow. As a general rule, however, terminals outside the United States are designed for shared use.

Since airlines compete vigorously in the United States, they are unlikely to agree willingly to share gates and other major facilities. But there may be exceptions. A number of locations feature many small operations that are hardly in competition. Such appears to be the case at Atlanta, for example, as Figure 6.12 shows. This is the kind of situation for which shared use ought to be considered, even in the United States. And shared or non-exclusive use of gates and other facilities does, in fact, exist at a number of North American airports.

G. A procedure for choice

The overall conclusion of this discussion is that the design of terminals should combine centralized, decentralized, and transporter concepts. Arguments about which of these three concepts is best – or should be adopted – are sterile if not vacuous. It is almost inevitable that a hybrid terminal of some degree is most suitable.

As a first step in determining what combination makes sense for a particular site, information should be gathered to help decide this issue. We should particularly attempt to define, especially since it is often not readily available, the pattern of variations in the traffic; the intensity of transfer between flights; and the volume of crypto-transfers for picking up cars and similar purposes.

Next, we should try to identify the approximate degree of hybridization that is most suitable for this location. To do this, we can apply the simple analytic models suggested in the preceding sections. We can first estimate the diseconomies of scale of central terminals, if any, and compare them with the costs of decentralization. Next, we can compare the local costs of transporters and fixed facilities and, by associating these data with information about the variability of the traffic, determine the proportion of transporters that appears reasonable. We can also use the formula provided to estimate whether the savings obtained through joint use of facilities are worthwhile.

These analyses will certainly be crude, but they can be helpful in screening out the most desirable configurations. The procedure also evidently requires extensive calculations and computers may be necessary to do the job. Even then, this design process is more oncrous than a simple intuitive selection of one of a handful of pure concepts. But the world is not so simple, and we must learn to deal with its full complexity.

Finally, we can use detailed analyses to investigate specific variations of the general configuration that appears best. At this point we can use the many factors which have been developed for sizing the specific dimensions that are necessary to service the expected traffic. This is the level at which most terminal design has been carried out, and is a process examined in the next chapter.

7 Sizing the Facility

As the preceding chapter indicates, airport planners have not done much systematic analysis of the shape and function of airport terminals. Indeed, the industry is only just beginning to recognize what questions need to be examined, which concepts ought to be implemented, in what combination. Intuition has been the deciding factor in the selection of the form of the terminals.

Planners have focused their analyses on a narrow portion of the design of airport terminals. They have a detailed methodology for calculating how big each component should be, once the larger question concerning the selection of the terminal has been decided. The approach rests on extensive experience and serves well for routine circumstances. But it has important drawbacks for dealing with situations that are not routine. As these cases are the rule rather than the exception, it is essential to understand the limitations of industry practice in the detailed design of terminals.

Over the years, airport planners have developed standard procedures for sizing the components of an airport. They are simple to describe. Forecasters first estimate the traffic that might prevail on some busy day in the future. The designers then multiply these numbers by some factors to calculate how much of each type of facility is needed to cope with the anticipated loads. The approach is evidently inaccurate because forecasting is so chancy, as Chapter 3 indicates, and requires much judgment in choosing satisfactory factors. But the approach proves satisfactory for sizing ordinary aspects of the terminals with which designers have a great deal of expertise, such as the area of waiting rooms, the width of corridors, the number of lavatories, and so on.

These procedures have not prevented airport designers from committing massive errors in sizing in some important areas, however. The automatic baggage system in the Pan American

Airways terminal at New York/Kennedy, for example, is too small by half, having apparently never managed to deal with more than two-thirds of the number of bags it was supposed to process per hour. Much the same proved true for British Airways' automated cargo facilities at London/Heathrow (which were recently removed), and for the computer-controlled conveyor belts for baggage at Paris/Orly. In all these cases, the design factors were probably wrong. Loads are often misjudged, too. The specifications for the design of the Airtrans trains for carrying people between terminals at Dallas/Fort Worth did not account for the inherent variability in the rate of arrivals of passengers, for instance, so the design could not provide the quality of service originally expected.

The sizing of essentially all new facilities has been plagued with problems. This has been especially true for automated systems. Indeed, the traditional approach typically fails just when airport planners most need guidance: when they have to deal with new situations, novel configurations of the terminal, unprecedented levels of traffic, and technical innovations.

These failures have occurred because designers either overestimated the capacity of a new type of facility or misunderstood the nature of peak loads. The root cause seems to be insufficient recognition of the peculiar nature of the behavior of service facilities operating near capacity. It is this characteristic we must understand if we are to avoid repetition of the errors in sizing that have haunted airport planners in the past.

A. Conventional practice

The American method for sizing airport facilities provides a good basis for exploring the deficiencies of prevailing procedures. It is well-documented and typical of approaches used elsewhere.[1] In brief, the process begins with an analysis of data from the busiest month of a recent year (generally the latest). From these statistics, forecasters determine the traffic that existed on an average day of this month and during the busiest hour of that day. They inflate these figures for the 'average-day-peak-month' and 'peak-hour-average-day-peak-month' to account for future expansions in traffic, and thus define the 'design day' and 'design hour' for sizing the facilities.

In the second stage, planners receive these data and typically further adjust them to incorporate their own guesses at future conditions. (The facility planners for one airline in the United States at one time routinely increased the forecasts by 50 percent!) The designers then finally multiply the resulting estimates of loads by empirical factors to calculate the number, area or capacity of the facilities required.

A key feature of this design process is that planners deliberately do not size facilities for the highest levels of the peak traffic. This represents a conscious, rational choice to sacrifice some of the passengers' comfort and convenience for the sake of economy. Indeed, the peak hour of traffic in a year occurs only about one-hundredth of one percent of the time; any facilities supplied to meet this load would thus be used at less than full capacity over 99·98 percent of the year. By designing for a lower level of traffic, such as for the average day of the peak month instead of the peak day of that month, airport planners may be able to reduce costs considerably with only a minimal penalty. Savings possibly up to 10 percent can be obtained at the expense of having people wait longer, or being more crowded, for a few hours of a few days in a year. Some balance between luxury and economy is admirable in concept.

The compromise represented by an 'average-day-peak-month' is suspect, however. Little evidence supports the notion that this choice of design loads strikes the best balance between comfort and cost. As the traffic on this day may be either close to that on the peak day or not, the potential savings may vary considerably. As this traffic may be either typical for the rest of the year or not, the service provided may or may not meet the desires of most passengers. Using the 'average-day-peak-month' approach, terminals for seasonal resorts might be vastly underutilized most of the year; whereas terminals for busy commuter stations, such as New York/La Guardia, might be too crowded for almost half the days of any month. Airports serving dissimilar traffic require a different tradeoff between efficiency and economy. No single design standard can possibly be fully adequate for all circumstances.

To define the best level of design, it is necessary to examine the detailed patterns of traffic throughout the year. This is because the overall quality of service provided by a design depends on the relative frequency of various levels of traffic, on whether the facility is underutilized much of the time or congested often. Such detailed analyses naturally require extensive calculations. Computers, however, facilitate the task considerably. We now can, and should, replace intuitive implicit choices about the cost and quality of service with explicit analyses and decisions.

A second important feature of the conventional process for sizing airport facilities is its reliance on fixed functions for dimensioning facilities. For example, it would estimate the required width of corridors as some specific function of the number of passengers per hour. This characteristic involves two related difficulties.

A first problem is that estimates of the capacity of novel devices are often far too large; their sizing functions are too optimistic. This failing appears to stem from a tendency to presume that machines can handle flows smoothly when, in fact, the inherent variability in the arrival of the traffic precludes this. Once recognized, the difficulty may be simply resolved by adopting a more conservative approach.

A second, more subtle problem is that the concept of the capacity of a service facility is somewhat meaningless. Its absolute capacity in a mechanical sense greatly exceeds its practical capacity to handle traffic on reasonable terms. This is because the quality of service provided by any facility depends upon the level of traffic: the more traffic, the more congestion, queues and delays. Its capacity in terms of the maximum amount of traffic it can process may, therefore, be significantly greater than its ability to handle the traffic with an acceptable amount of delay.

To overcome this second, most fundamental difficulty, planners must find a means to select the right factors for sizing. Here, no simple adjustment of previous practice is sufficient. We need to understand the complex interaction between the size of a service facility and its performance.

B. Behavior of service systems
Facilities that process variable flows of traffic behave in special ways that need to be carefully understood. As discussed in detail below, they all tend to create queues and cause delays

when the traffic is heavy. Furthermore, the situation rapidly worsens as the traffic comes nearer to the capacity. This behavior is characteristic of all manner of service systems: check-in counters for passengers; conveyors and sorters for baggage; corridors for pedestrians; runways serving arriving and departing aircraft; and so on. ˙

The operation of any service system is conveniently described by four measures: the rate of service it provides, specified by the design; the rate of arrival of the traffic to be serviced, mostly beyond the control of the planners; the length of the queues of traffic; and the average length of time it has to wait to be served. These last two indices determine the quality of the service.

The service rate – or capacity – of a system can be considered fixed, for any particular set of circumstances. Although it may vary in a number of ways as discussed subsequently, it is reasonably constant compared with variations in the arrivals.

The arrival rate typically fluctuates rapidly from month to month, week to week, and even hour to hour. As Figure 7.1

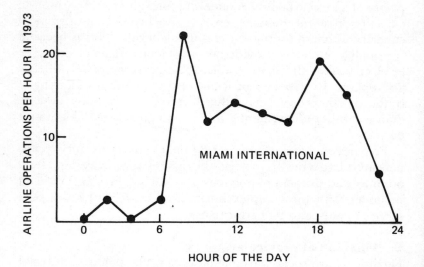

FIG. 7.1   Example of a daily fluctuation in aircraft operations at an airport

shows, it is quite usual for the number of aircraft operations to double within a hour or so, and the number of passengers and bags can be expected to change as fast.

Whenever the rate of arrivals exceeds the capacity or service rate of a facility, queues form and delays occur. Figure 7.2 illustrates this phenomenon. The graph on the left shows a rate of arrivals which exceeds the capacity of a service facility for a while. The consequences appear on the right: the service rate equals the arrival rate until it reaches capacity; it then is

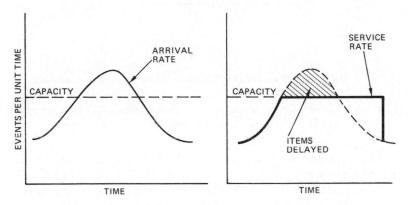

FIG. 7.2   Relation between arrival rate, service and delays at a service facility

constrained to be less than the rate of arrivals, thus causing the excess arrivals to queue up and wait; next, when the rate of arrivals drops below the maximum rate of service, the service rate remains high until all items in the queue have been processed; the service rate then drops down to equal the prevailing rate of arrivals.[2]

Queues and delays also occur when the overall rate of arrivals is less than the service capacity of a facility. This is due to the variability that may exist from minute to minute in the rate of arrivals, which causes the arrivals to exceed the service capacity at a specific time even though there is plenty of capacity overall. Whenever an aircraft arrives, for example, its passengers create a sudden demand for baggage service which cannot be met instantaneously. Even though ample capacity may be available to serve the average amount of traffic per hour,

delays will inevitably occur for a few minutes at a time. Figure
7.3 illustrates this behavior.

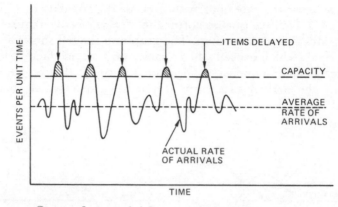

FIG. 7.3   Queues form and delays occur even when the average rate
of arrivals is less than the capacity of a facility

The amount of delay associated with a system operating
below capacity is most sensitive to how close the rate of arrivals
is to the capacity. When the arrival rate approaches the maximum rate of service, delays increase disproportionately faster
than the rate of arrivals. This is because the delay depends on
the frequency with which the instantaneous arrivals exceed
capacity, and this increases rapidly as the difference between
the overall capacity and the average rate of arrivals narrows.
Expressing the ratio of arrivals to capacity as

$$r = \frac{\text{rate of arrivals}}{\text{maximum rate of service}}$$

it can be shown that the total delay to arrivals is generally
proportional to $1/(1 - r)$.[3] This quantity becomes very large
as r approaches 1.

Extraordinary delays result, therefore, from any service
system operating near its capacity. Figure 7.4, showing a typical
graph of delays to aircraft waiting to take off on a runway (that
is, to receive service) illustrates this phenomenon. In recognition of this fact, designers should not plan to have systems
operate near their maximum capacity. As this quantity is

itself difficult to determine, responsible designers will, further-more, allow a substantial margin of safety between their antici-pated loads and their calculated capacity.

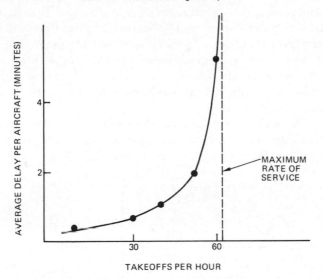

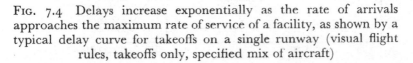

TAKEOFFS PER HOUR

FIG. 7.4 Delays increase exponentially as the rate of arrivals approaches the maximum rate of service of a facility, as shown by a typical delay curve for takeoffs on a single runway (visual flight rules, takeoffs only, specified mix of aircraft)

The performance of a service system will also be most unstable when operating near capacity. The variability of the length of the queues and of the delays is also proportional to $1/(1 - 1)$. Delays do not expand steadily as congestion increases. Instead, they fluctuate wildly, being small sometimes and absurdly long at others. This is the feature that is most intolerable to passengers and other users. It is quite impossible to determine in advance how long service at a congested facility will take, and users must allow for more time in their schedule than they actually need on the average. The unreliability of service systems operating near capacity is as important a problem as the delays themselves.

As a consequence of this behavior, airports and facilities with different patterns of traffic may create different levels of delay even though they handle the same flows on an average day. This means that the tradeoff between the cost of more capacity and the reduction in delay will not be the same for each situation: the facility with the greater peaks of traffic will benefit more from having more capacity. This in turn implies that providing the same level of capacity for situations that happen to have the same flow on the 'average-day-peak-month' (or at some other time) is inappropriate. On the contrary, the location with the more constant traffic requires relatively less capacity than the one with sharper peaks.

To see how this works out, consider Figure 7.5. This illustration shows the traffic for two hypothetical situations, both having the same level of traffic on the average day of the peak

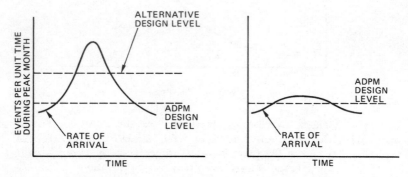

Fig. 7.5 Different levels of design may be suitable for situations with different patterns of traffic over time

month, but dissimilar patterns of demands. Suppose first that we create a design which provides enough capacity to meet the requirements of the 'average-day-peak-month'. According to the earlier discussion illustrated by Figure 7.2, it follows that this design causes many more people to wait when the peaks are sharp than when they are flat. Now imagine that we consider increasing the capacity at both locations to the alternative level shown in Figure 7.5. For the case where the traffic is constant, this leads to little reduction in delay and increase in convenience, and may easily not be worthwhile. But the change would reduce delays considerably where the load is peaked, and might be worth the cost.

The performance of a service system is, indeed, sensitive to the pattern of loads especially when they approach its capacity. The capacity of a service facility is, thus, not at all similar to our notion of capacity in everyday life, that is, the volume that a bottle or other vessel can hold. A bottle will accommodate any amount of liquid up to its capacity equally well; and after that, it can hold no more. A service facility, on the other hand, does not provide equal service at all times; its service rapidly deteriorates as traffic nears capacity. A service facility can, furthermore, eventually handle more than its immediate capacity by delaying traffic until an opportunity for service exists.

C. Measuring the capacity

Knowledge of the capacity of any facility and of facilities of various sizes is essential for planning. Designers need to be able to match facilities to the anticipated levels of traffic. But measuring the capacity of a service facility turns out to be a difficult proposition.

The problem is that the capacity of a service facility cannot be measured at all accurately. This follows from the essential nature of service facilities. Since delays and queues increase both very rapidly and unsteadily as the traffic approaches the theoretical capacity of a facility, as already shown in Figure 7.4, it is generally impractical – and sometimes impossible – to actually reach capacity. If we cannot be at capacity, we cannot know precisely where it is. Absolute capacity of a facility must, therefore, usually be estimated by some artificial construction such as asymptotic tangency to the graph of delays (as in Figure 7.4) or computerized simulation.

The difficulties in obtaining accurate estimates of absolute capacity are poignantly evident in the recent efforts of the US Federal Aviation Administration to develop measures of the ultimate capacity of various configurations of runways to service arrivals and departures of aircraft. Right from the start, it was obvious that actual experiments were neither practical nor economical. One could not hope to obtain all the aircraft needed to create the necessary levels of traffic, and to pay for them to wait in long queues for the situations for which the US Federal Aviation Administration wanted measures. So the government let a contract for an enormous computer simulation, requiring several years and about a million dollars to complete.[4] After reviewing the results, many people in government have severe misgivings about whether this has, or ever could have, fulfilled its expectations. When an effort of this size, with such knowledgeable backing, does not succeed, what can we expect for other cases?

The situation is further complicated by the fact that the capacity of a server is often sensitive to the precise nature of the traffic. Since different kinds of traffic interfere with each other, some combinations can be processed much more – and some much less – efficiently than others.

The long term efforts of the US Federal Aviation Administration to estimate the performance of runways vividly illustrate this sensitivity.[5] These analyses demonstrate for example, that a single runway can serve over twice as many small, general aviation aircraft an hour as a mix of commercial airliners. Airplanes of different sizes travel at different speeds and tend to catch up or fall behind and, generally, tend to interfere with each other's operations. The operation of jumbo jets also further reduces the capacity of runways. These aircraft create turbulent wakes that can be extremely dangerous: these vortices can literally flip over a large jet aircraft, as happened to a DC-9 landing behind a Boeing 747 in Texas. This phenomenon compels smaller aircraft to lag far behind the larger ones, and thereby lowers the number of operations per hour.

Traffic also flows more smoothly and rapidly through some arrangements than others. Two runways can serve half again as many aircraft when they are parallel to each other and placed far apart as when they intersect: aircraft can proceed more rapidly when their flight paths do not cross and when they thus do not have to wait for each other to pass.

Picking up from the previous discussion of the enormous variability in the performance of congested systems, it should also be pointed out that capacity can increase significantly as this variability decreases. For example, greater accuracy in air navigation systems would decrease the spread of arrivals at the end of a runway and increase capacity 25 percent, more or less, as Figure 7.6 illustrates.

As a general rule, a complex system will be able to serve a

wide range of volumes of traffic, depending on the situation. This fact creates an awkward problem for designers: not knowing what the future traffic will be, how can they determine what capacity their plans would provide?

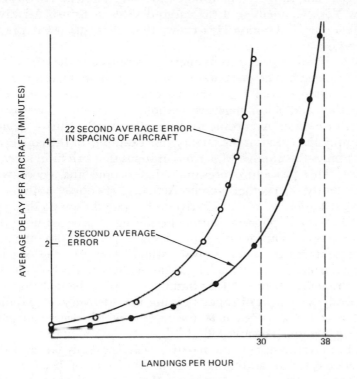

FIG. 7.6 Reduction in the variability of service increases capacity

In addition to these conceptual issues, planners must cope with a great deal of misleading information about the capacities of mechanical equipment such as conveyor belts, moving sidewalks, mobile lounges and the like. Manufacturers of equipment are perennially optimistic about the capabilities of their products and not infrequently overstate their effectiveness by 50 to 100 percent. As stated in a recent report on actual performance as compared to the supplier's statement of 'minimum capacities': 'As a general rule we believe that the moving sidewalk capacities listed in (the table of minimum capacities) are overly optimistic and that for planning purposes are half to two-thirds of that number of people can be moved per hour . . .'[6]

Much the same has been observed elsewhere. The automatic baggage handling system installed by Pan American Airways at New York/Kennedy and the cargo devices in British Airways' warehouses at London/Heathrow, that were discussed previously, illustrate the point.

Why is it that people so frequently overestimate the capability of equipment? The principal reason is that manufacturers tend to calculate capacity on the assumption that flows proceed smoothly and mesh together without interference or wasted space or motion. According to these estimates the rate of service is simply the speed of the facility (for example, of the conveyor belt) times the number of persons or items that can fit in a given space. This procedure presumes that people and goods will consistently fit together closely. Actually, of course, nothing of the sort happens. As items arrive to be served they go through an 'after-you-Alphonse' routine, hesitating to proceed until the other passes. This mutual interference produces an uneven, inefficient sequence of arrivals which prevents the service facility from delivering all it theoretically could. To cite the same report as before, '(Our findings) support the fact that the controlling element of capacity is not the "delivery" capability of the sidewalk as much as the rate at which users can gain admittance to the conveyor.'

The performance of automated systems is usually far less than calculated for an additional reason. Machines of any sort are poor at recognizing novel patterns; they thus tend not to be able to anticipate and avoid chains of failures, and seem unable to cope with unforeseen circumstances. The net result is that automated facilities often fail catastrophically. Furthermore, they frequently require standby equipment and human intervention to recover from such disasters. The net effect is often an embarrassingly low quality of service.

While the discussion so far has focused on the question of measuring the maximum capacity of a service facility at any time, this is not the whole problem. We need to know not only how well a design can cope with the peaks of traffic, but also how much traffic it will probably be able to accommodate over time. Because of the inevitable periods of slack demand for service, for example at night or during the off-season for tourist resorts, this practical capacity is only a fraction of what could be handled if the facility could operate fully at all times. Typically, the practical arrival capacity of a facility is 2000–3000 times its hourly capacity. These estimates must, however, be necessarily vague as they depend closely on the particular nature of the traffic at any place and at a given time.

These difficulties in measuring the capacity of service systems are not insurmountable. As in other situations with inherent uncertainties, planners and designers can proceed by using estimates, designing in adequate margins of capacity, providing alternative means of operation in case of excessive difficulties, and generally proceeding with a flexible strategy for the design and operation of the airport. Suggestions for how to do this follow subsequently.

D. Influencing the peaks

Since the peak loads largely determine how big a system should be – and, thus, how expensive it will be – it is important to see how they could be reduced. Sometimes, there is nothing to be done. For all practical purposes we cannot restrain fundamental forces of nature; we cannot steady earthquakes or stem the tides. But we may be able to influence loads which are created by man or society. In transport in particular, the loads and peaks of traffic are all induced by human choice, whether by shippers demanding service for their cargo or by passengers themselves. Here, the design and supply of facilities strongly affect the demand: poor roads and unsafe or unreliable public carriers discourage travel; good highways and service encourage movement, the dispersal of activities and more movement. The issues we face are, then: what should we do about the airport system to reduce peaks in traffic? How far should we try to reduce these peaks?

As in so many other instances, a proper statement of the problem defines the solutions. In this case the basic difficulty is that the users during the peak periods create disproportionately large costs for the system. They are, thus, generally subsidized by the other users and will impose an undue burden on them unless steps are taken to correct the situation. These subsidies from some users to others are both unfair and an indication of economic inefficiency. The most desirable strategy for controlling peak flows is to remove this inequity and eliminate this source of inefficiency.

The extra costs of peak users can be indicated by example. Consider air passengers traveling during the rush hours. They require facilities, such as gates for aircraft or areas in waiting rooms, that will be unused or unnecessary except during the four or five daily peak hours. Since this extra space receives relatively little use, compared to that required both during the peak and off-peak hours, it costs relatively more per passenger. Specifically, the cost per passenger of the extra facilities required for peak service must be more than the average. Furthermore, if the airport follows the typical practice of charging all users the same fees, regardless of when they use the services, the net result is that the users during the peak periods pay less than their fair share of the costs they create and everyone else pays more.

Peak period users of a service system also impose disproportionate delays on the system and place a burden on other users. This is because of the exponentially increasing relationship between the numbers of users of a service and their delays, as illustrated in Figure 7.4. The additional users who arrive during the peak period not only have to wait themselves but also raise the average wait for everyone else. They thus create delays in the system far greater than the average they incur themselves, and also directly inflict additional delays on others.[7]

Considering all costs and benefits, the most efficient strategy for dealing with peak loads is to charge users according to the full costs they impose upon the system. This implies that airport authorities should levy a surcharge on users during the peak periods to cover their extra costs. This approach is, therefore, known as the peak-hour pricing policy.[8]

The effect of instituting peak-hour pricing is to reduce the peak loads. This happens because the higher prices discourage some previous users from using the service. They decide that the value of using the airport during the peak period is less than its true cost, and that they should therefore use it at some other time or to go somewhere else for service. This is a rational, efficient economic decision. The airport and the users who really need and value service during the peak period benefit since they have neither to subsidize the traffic which has left, nor to suffer the congestion it caused.

Even small surcharges for using services at peak times can be remarkably successful. At New York/La Guardia a $25 minimum landing fee in the peak hours ($20 above the minimum prevailing at other times) was a principal reason for the proportion of general aviation traffic dropping from 52 to 18 percent. This led to a drastic reduction of the horrible delays that prevailed there in 1968.

Such easy victories may not always be at hand, however. Perhaps no users value their service lightly enough to be discouraged, or perhaps regulation has already sent them elsewhere. The peak-hour pricing policy that the British Airports Authority introduced in 1972 at London/Heathrow did not produce any spectacular results: the administrative expedient of refusing permission to schedule general aviation flights to Heathrow had already banished most of them, and quotas restricted commercial flights during peak periods. If these regulations had not existed, however, there is every reason to believe that the effect of the peak-hour pricing policy in London would have been as strong as in New York.

Quotas governing the number of users at any time or other administrative restrictions can also be effective in controlling peaks of traffic. But these methods are not efficient. There is no guarantee that such devices exclude those who least require the service nor include those who value it the most. Quotas, which ration service among the existing users, also discriminate against possible new users and uses. They restrict and delay the normal shifts in patterns of transport that should occur as a region develops and new opportunities arise as others fade. Basically, quotas are conservative, favoring the more powerful existing interests against newer and inherently weaker groups. This is a principal reason why quotas and similar devices are popular with administrators: they represent a policy that is far cheaper and more beneficial to existing users than peak-hour pricing. That does not mean, of course, that quotas are economically more efficient or socially more desirable.[9]

The peak-hour pricing policy has several significant practical advantages. It is, first of all, simple to administer as compared to any system of quotas. It does not require any procedures for deciding how to ration the quota, and thus eliminates extensive negotiations, arguments, and bureaucratic guerrilla warfare of all sorts. Second, as again opposed to any administrative restrictions, it produces income. This is a reason why peak-hour pricing is unpopular at first blush; but these revenues can be used to reduce costs elsewhere as they have at London/Heathrow. An airline that uses an airport continuously may, therefore, find that its costs stay the same or even decrease after peak-hour pricing starts. Finally, in contrast to alternative approaches, the peak-hour pricing policy involves a clear criterion for determining how far we should try to reduce peaks of traffic: the right amount has been achieved when the price charged the users during the peaks equals the total costs they impose on the system.

E. A guide to action
The discussion suggests that the planning of service systems should involve three distinct but related phases. First, the planners should obtain or develop an accurate description of the performance of the system under loads at various levels of capacity. Second, this information should be used to develop a plan for influencing peaks of traffic and, thus, reducing the overall level of investment required to implement a plan. Finally, it would be desirable – to the extent that it was practical and economical – to carry out an explicit analysis of the value of providing different levels of capacity instead of relying upon some arbitrary standard with hidden implications for costs and services.

In measuring the performance of a system, the essential objective should be to determine the relationship between delays and the loads on the system. This is a key basis for future planning, as it provides information needed to establish the right level of surcharges for a peak-hour pricing policy, and to carry out the analyses to determine the right amount of capacity to provide.

For systems which are already in operation at some location, direct measurements can be developed and many are already available. The greater difficulty arises with proposals for new kinds or sizes of mechanical devices. Unfortunately, in view of the probable continued expansion of air transport, planners may expect to encounter this problem frequently.

The performance of new service systems must be estimated carefully. In doing so we must first of all distinguish between the volume of traffic the new system might process if everything proceeded without interference (which is what manufacturers frequently label as the capacity of the device), and the actual maximum capacity the system could process, taking due account of all the inevitable interference. This second figure is what is needed.

As a rough rule of thumb, as suggested by the limited experience available to date, this actual capacity is about two-thirds of the ideal, unreal capacity. Once the analyst has made a judgment about the absolute capacity, estimates of the performance of the system with various loads can be made using the methods suggested by Figures 7.3 and 7.5 and the associated references. As any estimate about the performance of a new system will be unreliable, it would probably be good professional practice to apply a substantial margin of safety to allow for the various difficulties that will inevitably occur.

Turning now to the development of a plan for influencing peaks of traffic, we need two kinds of information. First, we must know the delays created by increases in traffic: this can be obtained from the measurements of the performance of the system under different levels of load. Second, we must also know how much investment would be required to increase capacity to cope with higher peaks. This second set of data depends closely on the details of the situation and must, therefore, be developed locally.

The analysis to determine the best level of capacity to provide should be pragmatic, above all. The issue is that any arbitrary standard for planning, such as that of the 'average-day-peak-month', is blind to the particulars of any situation and may, therefore, commit us to unnecessary and wasteful expense – or may cause us to skimp excessively on convenience. The effort put into the planning and design of any system should be in proportion to the improvements that might be expected. Just as it would be bad professional practice to accept standards unthinkingly, so it would also be reprehensible to do analysis for its own sake. Balance is required.

Throughout the process of sizing the terminals, planners should also be especially sensitive to how little anyone can know accurately about the capacity and performance of service systems. This means, in practice, that they have a responsibility to design their facilities with substantial factors of safety with regard to capacity. This is essential to providing adequate service.

In outline, this analysis should include a detailed description of the pattern of loads over time; a specification of alternative levels of design; and calculations determining the reductions in delay and costs associated with each alternative.[10] The exact procedure chosen and its levels of detail must depend upon the actual circumstances.

8 The Bottom Line

In planning the development of airports, we must ultimately evaluate the alternatives. We must in some way determine their advantages and disadvantages and, by weighing the pluses and the minuses, assess the overall desirability of each proposal. The questions are: what procedure should we use? How should we measure the value of any project? What rule should we follow to choose our strategy of implementation?

Any community inevitably has several, conflicting objectives for transport. On the one hand society desires economic efficiency. The public generally agrees that investments should be worthwhile and that it is the government's duty to conserve funds by getting the most value for money. This means that benefits should not only exceed costs, but be as large as possible. On the other hand, society is concerned about the equity of its decisions, about the distribution of the benefits and costs. A community may, for instance, think it fair to provide transport to all its members, even if some services do not pay for themselves. It may also not want to implement projects that benefit some at the expense of others.

Many of society's objectives inevitably conflict with each other. As numerous practical studies demonstrate, the allocation of resources that is most efficient economically almost certainly differs from the distribution we might prefer on the grounds of fairness.[1]

This inherent conflict implies that no single criterion for the evaluation of public enterprise will be universally acceptable. Efforts to find one are consistently unsatisfactory, as they must be.[2] Any choice – of a criterion or a project – represents at least an implicit compromise between diverse objectives and views. The extent to which this balance is satisfactory to anyone depends on their social values, their sense of the public interest, as well as on the facts of the case. No logical rule covers how such judgments should be made.

Both managers and planners of airports encounter similar conflicts over objectives, and a consequent inability to develop a single criterion for guiding policy. Indeed, their problems are closely intertwined. Management greatly determines when new facilities will be needed, and its prices for the use of an airport both modulate the demands to increase capacity and specify who is paying for the construction. Conversely, many of the costs of any project do not occur at the time of construction but over the life of the project, such as the noise of aircraft and the congestion of traffic on the airport roads, thus presenting problems for management. Management influences the planners' tasks, and vice versa. Taking planning and management together, therefore, let us examine the major benefits and costs associated with airports, and discuss the procedures that appear most appropriate for evaluating future developments and paying for existing facilities. First, however, let us look at prevailing practices and assumptions in the air transport industry.

A. Subsidy as a way of life

The air transport industry receives large public subsidies in almost all phases of its operation. It now regards this support as its rightful due and can generate powerful political opposition to any attempt to change this situation. This is a key observation. Proposals for policies of evaluation and pricing which do not recognize this fact are unlikely to be implemented. It is therefore essential that we understand the dimensions and extent of current subsidies.

Airlines often receive direct grants from the government. The United States, for example has paid over $1·26 billion from 1956 to 1975 (over $60 million a year on the average) to small, regional airlines to provide service on low density routes.[3] The British Government also makes substantial grants to its airlines from time to time. Quite recently, for instance, it gave British Airways some £50 million on the ostensible excuse that this represented their extra cost of operating British-made VC-10 aircraft, which they had been compelled to purchase instead of the more economical Boeing 707s. (It is not clear to what extent this was a grant to the airline or the manufacturer; it certainly was a subsidy to the industry.) Because direct payments appear in the national budget as payments to special groups, and thus receive considerable scrutiny from the government and legislators, they are generally low.

Air transport receives many highly valuable services at no charge or far below cost. National air traffic control systems typically serve civilian users gratis or close to it. These recurrent, annual subsidies can be substantial. In the United States, the national cost of air traffic control is about $1.5 billion a year or about 15 percent of the gross revenues of the commercial airlines. Even allowing generously that military and other official traffic incur about half this cost, and that should be paid directly by the public, the value of the service amounts to approximately $150 per flight or $3 per passenger.

The persistence of these subsidies is a demonstration of the political influence and power of the air transport industry. Attempts to make the users pay for air traffic control are repeatedly thwarted or diluted. In the United States, the airlines recently beat back government proposals to do this. They induced the Congress to amend the law requiring users to pay for airport services, so that it specifically prohibits the government from using user taxes to pay for air traffic control.[4] In Europe, Eurocontrol – whose existence as an international air traffic control system is at stake – has been so diffident about charging for services that airlines will not pay their full share until 1985, if by then.

Smaller airports characteristically fail to charge users enough for their services, and make up the difference from public funds. In Britain, all except the large London and Manchester airports have operated at a loss. In 1970, the deficit of these smaller airports was approximately £4 million, with municipal subsidies of over £2 per passenger at Liverpool and Teeside airports.[5] The situation is much the same for comparable American airports.

Conversely, air transport has been quite successful in not paying for the damages it imposes on others. Airlines have largely withstood pressures to install hush-kits on the aircraft they introduced in the 1960s, thus leaving thousands of people to suffer from jet whine. Except at a few airports such as Los Angeles and London/Heathrow, the airlines have managed to contain public reaction against blatant airport nuisances to minor restrictions on the number, time or direction of aircraft perations. Barring wilful misconduct, they have likewise ucceeded in limiting their liability to international passengers to a risible $16,000 per death ($75,000 if the flight connects with the United States).[6]

The hidden subsidies to air transport are the largest. They consist of tax exemptions, cut-rate governmental loans, and cross-subsidies from the profits on non-aeronautical activities. In the United States, for example, interest on money loaned to the airlines for the construction of airport facilities – by intermediary of municipal airport authorities – is free of national income taxes. The Government's loss is the airlines' gain. As explained further in Chapter 2, $560 million were raised in this way at Dallas/Fort Worth alone, indicating an implicit subsidy of around $20 million a year for just one airport. In France, the Government more explicitly loans money to the Aéroport de Paris at rates of only a few percent a year, far below its own cost of raising the money. Almost universally, airports escape real estate taxes and rates, thus gaining a further advantage.

At most airports, aircraft operators receive major cross-subsidies from other activities. Airport managements typically extract maximum profits from non-aeronautical sources such as parking lots, restaurants, duty-free shops, and so on. They then use these revenues to underwrite the cost of runways and related facilities and thus minimize their costs to the users. The amounts involved can account for a relatively large share of the income, as Table 8.1 shows.[7] Non-aeronautical revenues can, in fact, be large indeed: at London/Heathrow in 1974/75 they exceeded £25 million. In a crude aggregate sense the subsidies vanish since airport users as a whole pay the airport costs. The fact remains, however, that some users – people who use the

TABLE 8.1 *Revenues from concessions and rentals as a percent of total revenues for various airports*

Airport	Percent	Airport	Percent
Washington/National	69	Amsterdam	40
Los Angeles	51	Geneva	36
Paris/Orly	49	Frankfurt-am-Main	35
Zurich	44	Mexico City	35

restaurants, for example – subsidize other activities such as air cargo and air taxis.

The air transport industry has become so accustomed to subsidies over the years that it now acts as if it had a right to cradle-to-grave public support. The record in the United States, supposedly a center of competitive enterprise, is truly remarkable in this respect. Recent proposals by the airlines, by their lobby, the Air Transport Association, and by their regulatory agency, the Civil Aeronautics Board, have called upon the Government to pay for the development of new aircraft, most recently for short range aircraft but also for a supersonic transport; guarantee the airlines' credit in buying aircraft; protect manufacturers from bankruptcy, and to bail out Pan American Airways as they rescued Lockheed Aircraft Corporation; to create funds for the construction of airports, as through the Airport Development Program; to continue excluding further competition from any new airlines; and, on top of all this, to maintain the policy of trying to secure a 12 percent return on investment for the airlines. Much the same occurs in Britain and other countries where the Government owns airlines, airports and even the manufacturers.

To place this discussion in perspective, we should recognize that the patterns of subsidies became established many years ago when the aviation industry was weak. Historically, two principal reasons have justified subsidies to air transport. One is that vital national defense considerations require the government to develop aircraft and keep aircraft manufacturers in business by stimulating the markets for their products. The other is that the public interest demands that high speed transport be available throughout the nation or empire and, therefore, that the government should pay the airlines to insure the existence of this service. Forty, even twenty, years ago these reasons had great validity: military and civilian aircraft used similar technology; air transport might disappear without government support.

But the situation has changed. In most parts of the world, air transport is now a mature, powerful industry highly unlikely to disappear. It serves the pleasures of the holiday-makers and the more affluent as much as, if not more than, any vital national interest. It is time to reexamine the subsidy policies of the past.

What are the real benefits of aviation and airports? What are
their costs? Who should pay for what?

B. Economic benefits to the whole community?

Air transport is an essential feature of modern life. It is valuable
in commerce, enabling businesses to distribute products and
services further, faster and more cheaply. It is important to
vacationers who crave the opportunities for sun and adventure
it makes available. Access to air transport is logically part of any
plan for urban development. Airports not only provide this
service to a community, but may also attract new industry and
jobs. They are a vital feature of modern cities.

Proponents of airport development use such platitudes to
promote projects and generally wear down popular resistance
to the expense of constructing and operating an airport.[8] But
the issue of whether we should pay for an airport is not a question of whether it is an essential feature of modern life. So what
if it is? So too are schools, hospitals, roads, sewers and many
other public services for which society never seems to have
enough money. The real questions for any community are:
how much should it spend on each of its important services?
How should it allocate its scarce resources among the competing
demands, such as education and housing, as well as transport?
In assessing airport plans, it is not enough that they are
valuable. They must be sufficiently valuable to justify the
investment of public funds. Does money spent on them generate
more benefits to the community – more savings, jobs or growth
– than a like amount invested in alternatives?

Any estimate of benefits to a community is inaccurate under
the best of circumstances, since it is almost impossible to describe the exact effects of any system. For airports in particular,
accurate forecasts are especially rare, as noted in Chapter 3.
Furthermore, almost every group concerned with airports has
reason to overestimate their benefits for the public. Users want
better facilities at less cost to themselves. They are conservative
in calculating benefits to themselves, as any exaggeration in this
regard might encourage the airport authorities to raise their
charges. But they do have a strong incentive to be amply
generous in forecasting benefits to the community at large,
since these constitute the rationale for public subsidies to

airports.[9] Airports managers and governmental overseers of air transport themselves have a natural desire to extend their domain over a large system. Estimates of the benefits of airports to a region are thus almost unavoidably inflated.

Yet it is almost an article of faith among airport planners that airports significantly affect economic growth. The theme is pervasive and widely repeated in planning documents from all over. A couple of quotes from airport officials quickly give the flavor. 'I believe an entire community benefits because of an airport. I think that my city, Atlanta, has had tremendous growth *because* of the airport, and I do not feel it is proper to put the entire expense on the user. In other words, I think the general treasury should continue to fund various airport expenses.' And 'Air passengers and air cargo are, in fact, *the* catalytic agents providing stimulus for a *major* part of our economic stability and growth.'[10]

Saying it's so doesn't make it so, of course. The available evidence actually indicates that investments in airports have a modest effect on the local economy. To see why this might be, let us look at the situation closely.

Airports are said to improve a local economy in basically three ways:

(1) Better access and cheaper transport are especially effective in promoting local development;
(2) They generate several jobs and dollars of income off the airport, for each job and dollar spent at the airport;
(3) They increase the value of the land around them.

A kernal of truth exists here; these effects can happen. But to what extent will they occur in any particular case, and how much do they justify further investments in airports?

Access by air is clearly essential for some regions. Could the tourist industry of Miami – or Malta or Dubrovnik – have expanded as it did without airports to handle the tourists? Certainly not. In a few cases, some access to air transport is a necessary condition for development. But even then, the airports are not by themselves sufficient. Credit must be shared with many other factors. Without the sunny shores and cultural endowments, without investments in hotels and tourist attractions, Dubrovnik would have no tourist industry even with an airport. In fact, ample evidence suggests that the mere existence of an airport does little for a community. Both the United States and Britain are, for example, littered with dozens of former military airfields now available for civilian use: only a few have been associated with any perceptible economic growth.

Typically, a community already has some access to air transport, either through its own airport or nearby installations, and is considering whether to build new facilities. The locations where an airport might be the critical factor – sites which are richly endowed with attractive features and lacking all convenient access – are' extremely rare if not non-existent. The usual questions before the community are: how much does it stand to gain from greater access? And thus, what is its reason for subsidizing an airport, instead of letting the users pay?

Airport publicists commonly assert that greater access to air transport, and cheaper transport generally, attract new industry to a community. A plausible argument can be made to support this point of view: when the costs of distributing goods are lower, they become cheaper and more competitive farther away, thus broadening the size of the market. But the practical question is, whose market? The transport improvement that increases the attractiveness of a city as a location for new business, also makes it more vulnerable to domination from outside competitors. The community could hurt as well as help itself by improving transport. To what extent does a particular community gain on balance from greater access?

Smaller communities often suffer after transport has been improved. In the United States, for example, the construction of high-speed roads has drained rural communities throughout the country: people now bypass local shops to reach the better-stocked, more competitive stores of the larger cities.[11] As the UK Civil Aviation Authority put it,

> It is not necessarily the case that better transport links between metropolitan and peripheral regions serve to widen the market for the latter's products. Where the peripheral economies are largely complementary rather than competitive with the metropolitan region, that is, where they produce different rather than similar types of goods and services, this may well be so. But where ... the situation is one of

competition and, furthermore, where the metropolitan region is also able to offer a superior standard of service, the outcome is inevitably to the detriment of the provinces. Like free trade, good transport cuts both ways.[12]

Alternative ways of spending money may promote local growth more effectively. Whereas the benefits of investments in airports may flow principally to outsiders, the benefits of different subsidies can be retained locally. Tax holidays granted to new industry and money spent on the preparation of industrial sites can, for example, only draw industry into a town; they cannot profit industry elsewhere.

While present knowledge does not allow accurate predictions of how much industry investments in airports will attract, a clear presumption should exist against great expectations. On balance, these investments do not appear especially effective. Worse, they incur the risk that a smaller city may become not only an economic but also a cultural and political appendage to a major center.

Airport activities may intrinsically stimulate the economy. Airport promoters frequently allege that each job at the airport creates two to four times as many jobs in the local economy. The Port of New York Authority used to claim, for example, that the proposed fourth airport for New York would induce over 130,000 jobs. This is the multiplier argument. It says that the effect of any activity – jobs or spending – is multiplied several times. While this may describe some situations, the claim appears to be irrelevant to the decisions a community must make.

The multiplier argument is based upon the observations that several 'airport-related' jobs are associated with each job on the airport. A pilot, for instance, may require taxis to get home, their drivers need garages, whose mechanics have to buy groceries, and so on. True enough, activities at the airport are closely tied to the whole web of urban and regional activity. But as everything is connected, the argument is totally circular.

The association between jobs at the airport and jobs elsewhere does not mean that the former causes the latter. This is elementary. Logically, it is equally right to turn the question around and say that jobs elsewhere cause jobs at the airport.

And it may be closer to the truth. Careful examination of the
results of the extensive American aid for the construction of
highways throughout the world indicates, in fact, that local
development largely determines the use of transport rather than
vice versa.[13]

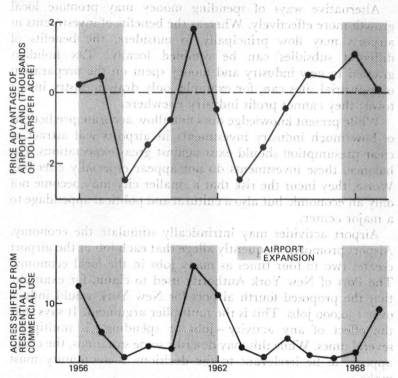

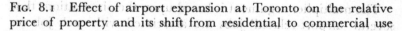

FIG. 8.1   Effect of airport expansion at Toronto on the relative
price of property and its shift from residential to commercial use

Nobody really knows how much economic activity might be
generated by investments in airport projects. The multiplier
effect possibly exists to some degree. But how much? Almost
certainly a new job at the airport does not create two to four
jobs elsewhere. Perhaps only a fraction of a job.

The multiplier argument, in any case, does not justify public
spending on airports. No evidence demonstrates that airports
create relatively more jobs than other activities – indeed one

may suspect they create less since they are capital intensive. As
public money spent on an airport is surely money not spent
elsewhere, decisions to develop airports are not likely to enhance
the employment prospects of a community. To a degree, this
choice merely favors one group over another.

Finally, developers sometimes suggest that airports raise the
value of the land around them. The centrepiece of this argument is Chicago/O'Hare: where twenty-five years ago the area
was virtually vacant, hotels, offices, and businesses now abound.
The price of land has risen as much as a hundredfold. But the
effects of the airport itself are speculative. A network of high-
speed roads was also built recently in the suburban area around
O'Hare, and has undoubtedly attracted many businesses.
Second, Chicago is a special situation; it is a turntable of air
transport in the United States, and a most convenient meeting-
place for persons spread across the country. Comparable development simply does not exist at most other airports; the
areas around those of Detroit, Pittsburgh, Copenhagen and
Rome are, for example, quite undeveloped.

Overall, investments at the airport do not appear to change
the value of the surrounding land significantly. They seem,
instead, to set off a complex interaction between the benefits
and disbenefits of the airport to its neighbors, in which the
attraction of the airport to commercial establishments counter-
balances the repulsion felt by residents who abhor the noise.
Figure 8.1 shows this for Toronto: each expansion of the airport
led to a shift of land from residential to commercial use; and an
immediate, short-term fall in prices of the land relative to
comparable uses elsewhere. As Crowley concluded, during each
expansion

noise-avoiders sell their residential property, driving down
the price . . . some land is shifted for other uses, thus, in turn,
bidding up the prices. The overall result of this process is
that relative land values ultimately end up about the same as
before . . . The important difference is that . . . the pattern of
land use changes substantially.[14]

What then is the net effect of airport expansion on neighboring property? Residents lose and new businesses pay dearly for
their space. The gainers, if there are any, are the developers

– or speculators – who manage to buy distressed residential
property, persuade the authorities to allow its use for business,
and sell it at a substantial profit. This is unlikely to be a process
the public will want to subsidize.

As far as the wider community is concerned, the major
economic effect of airport projects is to redistribute benefits.
Many businesses attracted to an airport could probably have
been located elsewhere. Jobs can be created by spending for
other purposes besides airports. Land made available to commerce is land denied to residential or agricultural uses. Sheer
economics does not seem to provide a compelling reason for
public subsidies to airports or their immediate beneficiaries: air
transport, its passengers, and other users. The justification for
subsidy, if it exists, lies in the desirability of specific redistribu-
tions of wealth and power.

Society may rightly wish to redistribute wealth or cater to
particular groups. Many public programs – in housing, education and other fields as well as transport – are based upon this
purpose. The government may want to promote social justice by
helping poorer regions, such as Appalachia in the United
States, or the Scottish Highlands; to carry favor with separatist
or political important regions, as by financing the development
of Montreal/Mirabel in Quebec or Dallas/Fort Worth in
Texas; or to strengthen militarily strategic areas, as Colombia
does by subsidizing air transport to the Amazon and Orinoco
basins. Such goals may be quite legitimate, but are not to be
confused with economic objectives.

C. Direct benefits

Let us now focus on the direct benefits of airports, resulting
from cheaper, safer, more reliable and convenient transport.
They basically come from two sources. The airfield and airways
installations, such as runways, taxiways and air traffic control
systems, facilitate the movement of aircraft, thus creating
benefits that accrue to the airlines or may be passed on to
passengers and shippers. The terminals and associated parking
lots, restaurants and stores that more specifically service the
passengers and other users generate profits that flow to their
operators or, more usually, are channeled to the airport
authority and spent on other activities.

The calculation of benefits is difficult to do accurately. While in principle the estimation of the benefits of a new facility is simply the multiplication of the savings it creates for each user and the number of users, less the costs, in practice the exercise is treacherous. Determining how many users will be helped is a first problem. In addition to those using the facility at present, more will appear due both to normal future increases in traffic and the more desirable facility. But as no one understands the behavior of users well, estimates of these increases are notoriously inaccurate, as indicated in Chapter 3.

A second problem is the lack of consensus on the values of many benefits. What is it worth to prevent a fatal accident or to save ten minutes of somebody's time? We can attempt to resolve this conundrum by estimating what the time, or life, might be worth if used productively; but the inherent assumptions that the savings are used intelligently (how is anyone going to use an extra few minutes?) and that productivity is a valid measure of human worth (are we prepared to advocate murder of the old and crippled?) debilitate this approach. Alternatively, we can observe what people pay to obtain similar savings, for example, when they choose to use a high-speed toll road rather than slower back roads. This approach presumes that people have complete information about their choices (a dubious proposition), and that they are buying the item of interest, say time, rather than the convenience of not getting lost or something else. It also supposes that a consumer's ability to pay for something equals its value to society; a proposition implying, say, that it is better to save the life of one millionaire than of a few hundred poor: an unlikely proposition for a democracy.

The best one can do under the circumstances is to estimate the size of the several benefits, and to suggest how they might be calculated for a particular problem. Feeble though this may be, it is an improvement over the more general practice of never really asking how much airport facilities might be worth.

The benefits of adding runways and taxiways, thus improving the flow of aircraft on the ground and reducing delays, are easiest to calculate. Well-known procedures exist for estimating the delays to aircraft in landing and taking off for a variety of configurations of the runway, types of air traffic control, and mix of aircraft, as indicated in the previous chapter. These facilitate the calculation of the time savings resulting from any new facility.

The value of reductions in delay depends on the type of aircraft involved and the number of passengers carried. Including all expenses, the jumbo jets cost around $1000 an hour, modern airliners about $700, and smaller aircraft correspondingly less. The passengers' value of time depends on who is flying; whether they are on business or on holiday; and their wages. In the United States it may be approximately $7·50 an hour. At busy airports, the cost of delay can mount up rapidly. At Chicago in 1969, for example, an estimated 2·7 million minutes were lost in delays, for a cost of about $30 million a year. Extreme caution should be exercised in interpreting such figures, however, as they are often exaggerated.[15]

The value of investments in air traffic control and navigation facilities is difficult to estimate. Instrument landing systems and similar devices prevent accidents and the closure of the airport during bad weather, events which depend closely upon the local climate and terrain as well as other factors. In the United States, where good facilities exist for landing in quite bad weather and low visibility, the costs of cancellation of flights and their diversion to other airports due to bad weather have been estimated to be between $10 and $30 million a year. Yet the British Government has apparently spent hundreds of millions of pounds on developing the capability to land aircraft in really extreme weather. To some informed observers, this has been as big a waste of money as the development of the Concorde.

Valuation of the benefits of reducing accidents and fatalities is complicated by strong emotions and general ignorance of what causes accidents at airports, or what can be done to prevent them. A few statistics, however, give a picture of the situation. Aircraft accidents now typically happen near the airport: one study of the United States indicated that three-quarters of all accidents and half of the fatalities occurred within five miles of the airport. Landings and takeoffs are the most dangerous parts of the flight. Airlines in the United States experience approximately 0·85 accidents and six deaths per 100,000 departures.[16] For a medium-sized airport handling 3 million passengers a year with about 100,000 departures, and assuming a value of $400,000 per death, the cost of human wastage amounts to several million dollars a year on the average. This gives some idea of what it might be worth to improve safety at an airport.

Extending the length of runways may reduce accidents and also open up the airport to heavier, more economical aircraft. Tentative analyses suggest that longer runways decrease the probability of pilots missing the runway or of landing hard, and reduce accidents by three or four percent for each extra 1000 feet of runway (within the usual range of about 5000–10,000 feet).[17] The extent to which the length of the runways limits operations depends on the particular circumstances of the airport and must be analyzed case by case.

The economic value of airport terminals lies principally in the services they provide for the convenience of passengers and shippers. Different arrangements and better equipment certainly can reduce the passengers' waiting time, and should be worth something, but this has essentially never been taken into account. The developers' have focused on the revenues from tenants. These revenues depend considerably on the local circumstances but may be handsome. Parking garages generate as much as 20 percent of an airport's revenues. In Europe, duty-free shops and concessions have ben extremely profitable for many cities. But no general rule prevails; it is probably best to estimate these benefits through discussions with developers and airlines who may understand the local commercial possibilities.

D. Costs

Costs, like benefits, are of two kinds: the direct expenses of the construction and operation of the airport, and the indirect burdens the airport imposes on the wider community. The latter particularly includes noise, the principal noxious side-effect of airports and the cause of many others, such as the potential devaluation of adjacent land.

The direct costs of airports are high. Airport terminals currently cost around $50 per square foot for smaller airports and $100 per square foot at larger cities. A major modern airport requires upwards of $100 million in capital investment and, for the largest new airports such as Dallas/Fort Worth or Montreal/Mirabel, closer to $800 million.

It is not practical to develop an accurate rule to estimate airport costs. The cost of any specific task varies over time because of inflation; from place to place due to geographic differences in climate, scope of the labor force, and so on; and due to the prevailing tax and economic climate. The 'Quarterly Cost Round-Ups' of the *Engineering News-Record* illustrate these differences clearly for the United States. The cost of the total airport is even more variable because of the dissimilar tasks and designs called for at each site. The large areas required for airports are frequently only available in places which are unoccupied because they are unattractive for other purposes, such as the Maplin Sands site (otherwise known as Foulness) for the third London airport. They typically require extensive preparation, by way of filling and leveling, to accommodate runways.

A budget for any project is, therefore, best put together through a detailed examination of the particular situation. As indicated in Chapter 3, even such knowledgeable analyses are inherently inaccurate. The real costs of an airport can easily be 25 percent greater than the original estimate, and it is not unusual for a runway, terminal or hangar to end up costing twice as much as anticipated.

Some general rules concerning the overall trend of costs may emerge however. Preliminary studies indicate that it may be possible to obtain reasonable information on the returns to scale. Specifically, the construction of large facilities with a repetitive design, such as runways or hangars, appears to exhibit economies of scale, meaning that the cost per square foot is smaller for larger projects. If true, this information would provide a useful guideline, indicating that these projects should be built somewhat in anticipation of future need, as one large project can be less expensive than two or more small ones at different times.[18] Conversely, however, some elements at the airport exhibit diseconomies of scale. As indicated in Chapter 6, facilities with intensive mechanization, such as automated cargo or baggage handling areas, appear to have this characteristic, implying that they ought to be designed around relatively small modules.

Estimation of the cost of noise is complicated by uncertainty over how to measure it. No formula can satisfactorily combine all factors which contribute to this nuisance. The aggravation is caused by the intensity of the disturbance; the mixture of different tones, high-pitched whines being more obnoxious than low rumbles; the duration of the disturbance; the number of disturbances; the time of occurrence, since being awakened at night is more bothersome than being interrupted by day; and so on. The United States, Britain, France, Germany and other countries have each developed several different ways of including these effects in a measure of noise. While each country has its favorite noise index, due to legislative or administrative preferences, there is little to choose between them.[19]

The procedure for evaluating the cost of noise is simple in principle. One needs to determine the distribution of noise created by an airport (known as the noise footprint), to project the number of people affected, and to assess the value of various levels of nuisance for each individual. The study of the UK Commission on the Third London Airport shows how this can be done in practice.[20] As an accurate estimate requires formidable computations, detailed analyses may not be worthwhile. This may be particularly so if the persons hurt are not to be compensated, and their annoyance is simply to be balanced subjectively against the benefits to users. In any event, the total cost of noise may be very large; perhaps of the order of several hundred million pounds for the major urban airport of London/Heathrow.

It should be pointed out, in fairness, that the level of aircraft noise around airports should decrease in many areas as new aircraft are introduced. The early jets, such as the Boeing 707s and the Tridents, produce a particularly aggravating sound. Engines on more recent aircraft, such as the Lockheed Tri-star and the Douglas DC-10, eliminate much of this whine by using a different configuration of the compressors. Aircraft operations will thus become comparatively quieter as the older aircraft are replaced by new ones which meet the current regulations on noise in the United States and Britain.

It is also conceivable that the government might force the airlines to retrofit aircraft engines with quietening devices. But as these 'hush-kits' cost anywhere from $150,000 to $2,000,000 per aircraft, depending on the approach used and the type of engine, and as the worst of the problem is going away with time, this appears unlikely.[21]

E. Evaluation

Several basic approaches are available for evaluating plans for a system. Cost-benefit analysis is the simplest. Modified to account for uncertainty, it leads to the procedures of decision analysis, as indicated in Chapter 3. Finally, elements of the community can be called upon to exert their influence in a negotiation process.[22] Each approach has a valid application at different stages of airport systems planning.

Cost-benefit analysis basically adds up all the costs and benefits of a proposal, considers either the size of their difference or their ratio, and evaluates the project according to that single index of merit. To do this, it has to presume that price – or at least people's willingness to pay – is an appropriate measure of value; that reasonable prices can be attached to all significant consequences of a plan; and that consensus can be obtained on these prices. These assumptions are most closely met for projects with obvious economic implications, whose benefits and costs fall on the same persons. Problems involving the extension of runways, or the addition of taxiways may fall into this category. Assuming no negative effects on any neighboring community, the users of the airport both receive the benefits of easier travel with fewer delays, and pay for them through higher landing fees on their aircraft. Cost-benefit analyses have been most successfully applied in such areas.[23]

Decision analysis is a refinement of cost-benefit analysis which focuses particularly on the uncertainty that surrounds many problems. The idea here is to consider the full range of possible results and to weigh their importance according to their likelihood of occurrence. It has the great advantage of not polarizing around 'average' possible outcomes that are, in the event, not too likely to occur. For the planning of the Mexico City Airport and elsewhere, it has been useful in the development of long-range strategies by uncovering immediate actions that preserve future flexibility at least cost.[24]

Cost-benefit analyses may be inappropriate for many larger issues. They simplistically presume that the effects of complex plans, with extensive ramifications for diverse sections of society, can be meaningfully represented by a single number. The approach takes no account of the distribution of benefits and costs, of whether those who bear the brunt of the costs have any connection with those who benefit. As Mishan put it

> in such economic calculations *equity* is wholly ignored. If indeed the business tycoons and the Mallorca holiday-makers are shown to benefit, after paying their fares, to such an extent that they *could* more than compensate the victims of aircraft spillover (noise), the cost-benefit criterion is met. But compensation is *not* paid. The former continue to enjoy the profit and the pleasure; the latter continue to suffer the disamenities.[25]

A procedure so blind to obvious inequities is not likely to produce recommendations acceptable to a democratic community, especially when many people might be called upon to suffer from a decision.

The attempt to determine the location of a third London airport by cost-benefit analysis was unsuccessful largely for these reasons. The method simply had no mechanism to account either for inequities or other planning considerations, such as the desire for open space around London, that cannot be measured and priced. When all the sums were totted up, the public and the Government realized that the recommendation was antagonistic to basic goals and concepts of fairness and, therefore, had to be rejected.

The evaluation of important projects with substantial, differential impacts on various groups requires an understanding of the distribution of these effects. We should both assess the size of the potential impacts of a proposal and tabulate their incidence on significant groups of society. With such information we can consider not only the economic efficiency of a project, but also its equity.

What a community may make of this information depends upon its modes of social choice. In the United States, a variety of interest groups are likely to exert pressure in the political processes that lead to a decision. Elsewhere, public choices emerge in other ways, as discussed in Chapter 2. The French may try to determine a 'fair' solution rather arbitrarily according to a mixture of expediency and some measure of social optimality. In Britain, as illustrated by the polemics over the third London airport, decisions concerning large social enterprises result from an ambivalent combination of cost-benefit arguments and political pressure.

F. Paying the costs

The conflict between equity and economic efficiency carries over from evaluation to the matter of paying for facilities. The general principle, endorsed both by the International Civil Aviation Organization and most airports, is that each type of traffic should bear its fair share of airport costs. But it is not obvious what either a 'fair share' or 'airport costs' might be specifically. Consequently, as the British Airports Authority put it, 'in the absence of any clear and defensible charging policy, consultation between an airport and its airline customers about the structure and level of its charges often comes to resemble a form of guerrilla warfare.'[26]

This argument between the airlines and users on the one hand, and the airport and the general public on the other, has two basic dimensions. First, it concerns the overall level of payments: should the airport be subsidized by the public, break even, or be a profitable enterprise? Second, it revolves around the division of these payments between the airlines, general aviation, and other users.

As regards the overall level of charges, economic efficiency demands that, as discussed in Chapter 7, users be charged the incremental cost they impose upon the system. This amount is the sum of the direct costs they create and the costs – or benefits – they indirectly induce in the other users.[27]

The amount an airport might receive by applying this principle may have little relation to its total costs. Suppose, for example, that increased air transport benefits the users – and society generally – because higher frequency reduces delays. Maximization of total benefits to all concerned requires that users be charged for their direct costs on the airport, less the value of the time saved. By following the criterion of economic efficiency, the airport would then find itself, in this case, subsidizing the users.

This result may not represent a fair distribution of costs from society's point of view. No logical resolution exists to this essential conflict. In practice, some compromise has to be adopted. The nature of this adjustment depends on the extent to which society feels that payments from the public treasury to the users of air transport, or vice versa, are in the public interest. Some general guidelines can be outlined.

The justification of a subsidy, from an economic point of view, lies in the value society places on the increase in air traffic. This may be high in remote or sparsely inhabited regions where the provision of daily flights is important because of society's desire to link all regions of the country. A presumption in favor of subsidies may thus exist for small, infrequently visited airports in such places as Alaska or the Outer Hebrides of Scotland.

Conversely, when increases in air traffic increase costs to users, a negative subsidy is justified – that is, a tax on the users. This situation occurs when the airport is congested, as explained in the previous chapter. A policy of economic efficiency may then result in a net payment from the users to the public. But the dichotomy between economic efficiency and equity is easier to resolve for profits than for losses. This is done by taking advantage of the variability of air traffic. The profits obtained from periods of peak traffic can be used to lower the charges during periods of infrequent service, when a subsidy might be desirable. This is the policy adopted explicitly by the British Airports Authority for London/Heathrow and implicitly by the Port Authority of New York and New Jersey for the New York airports.

For airports with neither so little traffic as to justify a subsidy, nor so much as to warrant an overall tax, the preferable solution is for users to pay their full costs. This approach satisfies the criteria of both economic efficiency and equity. It is to be noted in this connection that full costs should include the value of the capital invested in the airport. This is equal to its value in alternative uses, typically equivalent to an annual rate of interest, net of inflation, of 10 percent or more.[28]

As regards the division of payments between the users, most airports have adopted policies that are inconsistent both with economic efficiency and equity. Under pressure from the airlines and the International Civil Aviation Organization, they follow the general rule of extracting maximum profits from customers for their ground services, such as parking garages, restaurants and so on; while charging as little as possible to the operators of aircraft.[29] The profits drawn from some users go to pay the way of others. These sums can be considerable; parking charges alone may account for 20 percent of an airport's revenues. And the rate of return airports can extract from some users is truly exorbitant: typically car rental agencies in the United States pay 10 percent of their gross income – often exceeding $1 million a year – for the privilege of having a few counters and parking stalls. The arrangement is inequitable, as some passengers, renters of cars say, pay a tax of $5 per trip so that other forms of traffic, say air cargo, can pass through the airport at two-thirds of its real cost. It is also economically inefficient since it discourages some valuable forms of use while encouraging traffic that, by definition, does not pay its full costs.

The political power of the airlines and aircraft owners will almost certainly prevent a correction of this imbalance anytime soon. Permanence does not, however, imply that prevailing policies for the division of airport costs are desirable. They are not. The public would benefit from a more equitable system.

So far we have only discussed pricing policies. But they only represent one way – although a major one – of distributing costs. Costs can also be transferred between users and the public, or between classes of users or sections of the public, by various forms of regulation.

Regulation imposes costs on some elements of the system for the purpose of benefiting others. The rules governing the operation of aircraft near airports surrounded by residential areas illustrate this. The peculiar maneuvers necessary to reduce noise over critical zones, and thus to benefit their inhabitants, increase the costs of operation of the aircraft. The aircraft may, in extreme cases, have to take off without a full load of fuel or passengers with a consequent cost of several thousand dollars per flight involved.[30] Curfews or quotas limiting the operation of aircraft at night, such as exist at Paris and London, similarly reduce nuisances to local residents by forcing airlines to schedule flights at less convenient times, requiring more crews or aircraft and thus increasing costs.

Quotas governing the number of flights at an airport result in a transfer of costs between airlines. These rules, which exist at London/Heathrow and Washington/National, for example, typically permit the airlines that already serve an airport to operate a fixed number of flights. Airlines wishing to expand their services or to come in are effectively frozen out, barring major political pressure. The quota then works to lower the congestion and its costs to some airlines, while denying revenues to others.[31]

Finally, the British rules establishing the so-called 'minimum noise' routes for flights near London/Heathrow illustrate how regulation can redistribute costs between sections of the public. The flight paths created by this principle concentrate all traffic – and noise – over particular, unfortunate areas of the city. Some sections are relieved of a burden through the unwilling sacrifice of others.[32] Such regulation is as effective as any form of pricing in making people pay the cost of airports. Whether it is equitable is a matter to be decided locally.

9 Epilogue

The Air Transport industry is passing through a period of profound change, as the writers of both prefaces have emphasized. This evolution requires a major reorientation of attitudes and expectations, and a major redirection of the focus of our concerns. The economic and social costs of airports are now very high, and place considerable constraints and responsibilities on airport planners. They can no longer presume to design airports in isolation, either from each other or from the urban and regional communities they serve. Nor can airport planners continue to expect that rapid growth and a generous public will afford them ample freedom as to what they build or do. We must now all learn to plan airports as integral parts of a larger system, and to face stringent economic and environmental realities.

This work is an attempt to help define how we might develop airport systems planning. What this should be is neither clear nor will be for some time. Proceeding on the premise that a good question is half the answer, I have tried to suggest some ways to consider the future of airport systems planning. My main hope is that I will stimulate others to understand the problems of air transport and airports better, and to revise and extend the concepts presented in the book.

Many of the specific suggestions I have offered will inevitably turn out, after the fact, to have been misguided. I apologise in advance for these errors, and trust that readers will accept that they are inevitably part of any effort to identify future problems and needs. Definitive monographs can, after all, only be written after all the results are in; they are the epitaphs for activities that have ceased to change!

As each chapter indicates, there is much we do not know about airport systems planning. Future work would profitably concentrate on some of these issues:

(1) What are the elements that limit the transfer of technology and its applicability between different cultures?

(2) What combinations of methods will be most effective for forecasting, and what procedures should be adopted to develop strategies for uncertain futures?

(3) How do the different elements of the air and ground transport interact, and how do people choose between them?

(4) What combination and size of facilities best serve a heterogeneous, fluctuating traffic?

(5) How should we pragmatically balance fairness to all elements of the community and economic rationality in paying for airports?

I look forward to working with colleagues throughout the world on these issues. The faster we can get on with the job, the better: failure to adapt to the new conditions bears a heavy cost for all.

Richard de Neufville
December, 1975.

Notes

Chapter 1

1 Stratford (1973) conveniently summarizes the evolution of air transport up to the early 1970s.

2 The US Department of Transportation (1974) reports that in 1971 individual states anticipated spending annually an average of 1·34 billion in 1971 dollars, equivalent roughly to 1·7 billion in 1976 dollars, on airports between 1972 and 1990. The Department itself, as of 1974, thought anywhere from a third to a half of this might be sufficient. The Dallas/Fort Worth Airport cost around $800 million.

3 The current procedures for airport planning rely extensively on publications of the US Federal Aviation Administration, the International Civil Aviation Organization, and the International Air Transport Association, as described by Horonjeff (1975). Young and Nemec (1974) provide a critique of the relevance of these procedures.

4 US DOT (1974).

5 UK CAA (1972).

6 de Neufville and Marks (1974) present numerous practical examples of the fruitful application of systems analysis to the planning and design of large, complex projects.

7 The quotes are from Rittel and Webber (1973) and Webber (1973), respectively.

Chapter 2

1 See, for example, the publications of the International Civil Aviation Organization (1969 and various other dates), the International Air Transport Association (various dates) and the US Department of Transportation, Federal Aviation Administration, jointly with the Airport Operators' Council International (1970).

2 This quote is from the ICAO Aerodrome Manual Annex 14 (various dates). The next is from the June 1974 issue of *Airport Forum*.

3 The US plans provide data for implementation of the Airport and Airway Development Act (US Congress, 1970). The

French plans appear as part of each five-year plan for the nation. See, for example, US Department of Transportation, Federal Aviation Administration (1973) and France, Commissariat Général du Plan, Commission des Transports (1971). In Britain, a national airport plan is being developed, and may be announced by 1977: UK Civil Aviation Authority (1972; and 1975 a, b, c).

4 See UK Department of Trade (1975, 1976).

5 UK, Cmnd. 3437 spells out this policy. It requires that the rate of return equal the prevailing opportunity cost of money, defined to be at least 10 percent a year. The British Airports Authority's annual reports describe its own experience, which should be read keeping in mind that it has received over £120 million in Government loans at 5¼ percent interest. Doganis and Thompson (1973) calculate recent rates of return for other UK airports. UK CAA (1975 a, b, c) outlines current UK policy on uneconomical facilities.

6 The best comparisons of the three countries are probably those of Shonfield (1965), Cohen (1969) and Rose (1969). Avril (1969), Parry (1969), Massé (1965) and Clawson and Hall (1973) describe the functions and objectives of these governments.

7 This discussion draws on Meyerson and Banfield (1955).

8 Manheim (1974) and Baram (1974) discuss recent American practice with regard to the planning of transport projects and constructed facilities.

9 Quoted from Block (1975).

10 Beesley (1973) describes and the UK Commission on the Third London Airport (1970, 1971) illustrates the principles of social cost-benefit analysis.

11 The UK Noise Advisory Council (1971) established this policy, which Hart (1973) reviews in detail.

12 Wheatcroft (1956) provides the best available description of the largely secret organization of airline pools.

Chapter 3

1 For a description of the American master planning process for airports, mandated by the government for all airport authorities that wish to be eligible for national financial support, see the US Department of Transportation, Federal Aviation Administration (1971). The International Civil Aviation Organization (1969) publishes the standard international manual for airport master planning.

2   The lack of traffic has forced the Airport Board to raise the landing charges from \$0·83 to about \$1 per 1000 pounds in order to pay its bonds. Meanwhile the automatic train system has cost three times the original estimate and performs at a standard which induced airlines to bypass it for baggage transfers, their employees to demand and obtain a special bus service, and the Postal Service to abandon the system.

3   The UK Commission on the Third London Airport (1970, 1971) documents these efforts. See particularly Appendix 7 of their Report on 'Timing of the Need'.

4   Formally, the principle is that the sum of the standard deviations of the parts is greater than the standard deviations of the whole, so long as the parts are not positively correlated. That is, for example, $S_x + S_y > S_z$ for $x + y = z$, since $S_x^2 + S_y^2 = S_z^2$. This implies that the percentage changes in the parts can be expected to be greater than the percentage changes in the whole.

5   Haney (1975) reviews these forecasts and methods, for which see the US Department of Transportation, Federal Aviation Administration, Office of Aviation Economics.

6   The Port Authority of New York and New Jersey, formerly the Port of New York Authority, for which see (1957) and (1970). See the Port of New York Authority (1965) and Howard and Augustinus (1974) for a description of the kind of detailed data they use.

7   See UK Commission on the Third London Airport (1971).

8   Technically, this approach is a form of econometric modeling, a process which has been reasonably successful in national economic planning and other endeavors for which theory is well-developed and validated. As regards transport, however, the theory is still quite weak. We so far have little real knowledge about which combination of factors impel people to go somewhere or to choose a particular mode of travel. Models of the demand for services thus commonly consist either of simplistic analogies between human behavior and physics, as with the 'gravity' models of human interaction; or of procedures to maximize abstract and unsubstantiated notions of the 'utility' or value individuals might place on services. No amount of mathematical genius can overcome these basic conceptual limitations. The argument is not against econometrics in principle, but against its wanton application in large doses where it is inappropriate.

9   Howrey (1969) documents this point extensively, and Haney (1975) also discusses it.

10   The standard references on technological forecasting are Martino (1972), Ayres (1969) and Jantsch (1967).

11   The US Federal Aviation Administration has generated annual forecasts for each of the following six years. We compared these projections with what eventually happened to obtain a record of the differences. Multiplying the standard deviation of this distribution by 0·7 gives an estimate of the 50 percent confidence limits on the error. Kiernan (1970) compiled the graphical comparisons of the forecasts. Besse and Desmas (1966) obtained similar results.

12   Moore (1973) carried out the survey of estimates of the elasticity of the demand for air travel which led to Figure 4.2. The Forecasting Manual of the International Civil Aviation Organization (1972) tabulates additional examples of the range of estimates.

13   As reported by the International Civil Aviation Organization (1972).

14   The US Federal Aviation Administration, Bureau of National Capital Airports (1962) prepared these forecasts.

15   Data on passengers and aircraft operations are available for practically any airport. For a convenient source for larger US airports, see US Department of Transportation, Federal Aviation Administration (1974).

16   See Port of New York Authority (1950) and (1958) for the forecasts. For data on the actual traffic, see Port Authority of New York and New Jersey (Annual).

17   Systems Analysis and Research Corporation (1968) prepared the forecast for the Port of Oakland.

18   Knudsen (1976) obtained the data for Figure 3.6 from records of the US Federal Aviation Administration. Merewitz (1973) reports similar findings for a wide variety of civil engineering projects.

19   The articles by de Neufville and Keeney (1973, 1974) describe the Mexico City case in detail. They and de Neufville and Stafford (1971) provide an introduction to the strategy of decision analysis.

Chapter 4

1   See UK CAA (1975a).

2   Wilson (1973) provides a brief, incisive picture of the Concorde and its economics.

3   The data plotted in Figure 4.1 came from the US Immigration and Naturalization Service, which counts all entrants to the

United States from overseas. This includes all the crews from cargo vessels. This is why the recent data are not as close to 100 percent as one might suspect.

4 Jego (1975) studied this phenomenon in detail.

5 The British Airports Authority has, for example, reported profits of upwards of 17 percent on the facilities invested in London/Heathrow and Gatwick. The Swedish Government reportedly has had a similar policy of raising taxes through landing fees.

6 Park (1966) studied the Detroit case, using data from Brown (1965). Bower (1974) documents a similar effect associated with the shift of commercial flights from Houston/Hobby to the less accessible Houston International Airport. Genest (1970) analyzed the accessibility of different locations and the Chicago case.

7 Southwest Airlines only serves the State of Texas. As an intra-state carrier it does not have to report to the US Civil Aeronautics Board so that conventional data are unavailable. These figures are from the Wall Street Journal, August 4, 1975.

8 See US Congress, House Committee on Interstate and Foreign Commerce (1969) and US Congress, Senate Committee on Commerce, Subcommittee on Aviation (1969).

9 The quote is from UK CAA (1972). For the use of the concept for Oakland, see the Systems Analysis and Research Corporation (1968).

10 de Neufville *et al.* (1972) report on the Cleveland situation, and the evidence on catchment areas comes from Gelerman and de Neufville (1973) and British Caledonian Airways (1975).

11 The evidence on the S-shaped behavior comes from many sources. See in particular de Neufville and Gelerman (1973), British Caledonian Airways (1975) for UK statistics, and Fruhan (1972) for a description of views of the air transport industry.

12 Yance (1971) documents this phenomenon.

13 Block, the planning director for the Aéroport de Paris during the development of Paris/de Gaulle, expounded this view repeatedly in conversation.

14 Gordon and de Neufville (1973, 1975) discuss the concentration of airline traffic and present methods for calculating the optimal patterns of service. The measure of concentration used in Figure 4.8 is Gordon's index. Rusconi-Clerici (1976) presents data on shifts in transfer rates, obtained following the procedure outlined by footnote 3 for Chapter 5.

15 The data in Figure 4.7 came from the 1965 Congressional Hearings concerning this dramatic change in the airline network. These were the first of many. See US Congress, Senate Committee on Commerce (1965, 1970, 1973, 1975). The quote comes from the 1973 Hearings.

16 From De Vany and Garges (1972).

Chapter 5

1 Bauml (1974) covers the recent experience in the United States with regard to parking fees. Doganis and Thompson (1973) review current practice in Britain.

2 Chapter 2 outlines the fundamental national differences that influence airport planning, and Chapter 8 describes various arrangements for paying for airport facilities.

3 Although the number of transfer passengers has important implications both for the demand for airport access and for the design of airport terminals, it is not generally available. It is not generated routinely as a by-product of some necessary activity, such as financial accounting or the preparation of passenger lists. The number of transfers at any airport has to be either obtained from special surveys or estimated from other data. Data in Tables 4.1, 5.1 and 6.1 result from a comparison of the numbers of passengers originating from a city and emplaning at its airports, as given by the Origin-Destination Survey of Airline Passengers (US, Civil Aeronautics Board, quarterly). While this is currently the best method to obtain these statistics in the United States, it is unfortunately inaccurate for many reasons: the data are limited, covering only passengers on domestic, scheduled flights; they are incomplete, since they do not collect data from major intrastate airlines in California, Florida, Hawaii and Texas, which are independent of CAB regulation; their totals are systematically biased, giving figures from 5 to 25 percent less than those reported by the CAB on its ER-586 Report and in the Airport Activity Statistics (US CAB and FAA, semiannual); and they are notoriously full of miscellaneous errors. Considerable care is needed to obtain any reasonable estimates of transfers at an airport.

4 Many surveys of airport traffic have been conducted. They are not strictly comparable because of differences in definitions, scope and conduct of the inquiry, etc. Also, they are usually inaccurate. de Neufville, Skinner and Koller (1971), Sutherland (1969) and Bovy (1969) compare the results for the US; and Russell and O'Flaherty (1969) for Europe.

5 Using repeated surveys of how passengers responded to changes in fares and schedules on access trips to New York airports in addition to other evidence, MIT investigators found that the price elasticity for the choice between alternative modes of access is about −2, whereas the elasticity with respect to travel time is only about −1. de Neufville (1973) describes this work.

6 Technically, the cost-effectiveness analysis identifies the dominant or Pareto-optimal set of possibilities. Depending upon how one thinks of it, these solutions define the cost-effectiveness function, or equivalently, the transformation curve. The slope of this curve at any point corresponds to the value of the service, in our case the value of time, implied by the solution.

7 See Voorhees (1966) or Whitlock and Cleary (1969).

8 This discussion summarizes the detailed report of de Neufville and Mierzejewski (1972).

9 The UK Ministry of Transport (1970) demonstrates the advantages of connecting Heathrow to the Underground. Despite the fact that rail connections to the airport can only be economical as part of a comprehensive regional scheme, it is interesting to note that the new Montreal service is still billed as an airport system: the Mirabel-Montreal Airport and Regional Rapid Transit.

10 For an extensive analysis of the usefulness – or lack of it – of consolidation of air cargo, see de Neufville, Wilson and Fuertes (1974).

11 Tilles (1973) gives a general discussion of this topic. A special procedure for estimating what is required and detailed data for London/Heathrow is available from IATA (1975).

12 Whitlock and Sanders (1974), Hurst (1974), Voorhees (1966), Bovy (1969) and Russell and O'Flaherty (1969), provide data on parking.

Chapter 6

1 Kanafani and Kivett describe this typology in Chapter 9 of Horonjeff (1975), and the joint report of the Parsons Company and the Air Transport Association of America (1973) analyzes it. Since the ATA is a representative of the major US airlines, its report reflects their particular interests. These cannot be presumed to be congruent either with those of other countries or even different elements of the community within the United States. Its report must be viewed accordingly, and its findings recognized as controversial.

2   Transporters are also called mobile lounges in North America. This term is really a misnomer since it is inefficient to use vehicles as lounges; they and their drivers should be in use, moving passengers to and from aircraft, as much as possible.

3   The current dominance of architects in the design of terminals is suggested by their responsibility for the available textbook treatments of the subject: Kivett (with Kanafani) in Horonjeff (1975), and Blankenship (1974); as well as by the architectural focus of Sommer (1974).

4   Data are also often subject to systematic biases. At smaller airports it is not uncommon, for instance, for the statistics on aircraft operations to be distorted upwards: flight controllers get higher pay when their workload increases. The opportunity to fiddle with the numbers is tempting.

5   See Footnote 3, Chapter 5.

6   These figures come from the annual reports of British Airports Authority, the Port Authority of New York and New Jersey, the Aéroport de Paris, Flughafen Zurich, etc. Most airports maintain records of this sort even if, as for Los Angeles, they do not publish them.

7   See US DOT, FAA, Office of Aviation Economics, Aviation Forecast Division (semiannual).

8   The Aviation Week and Space Technology Magazine reports data on the punctuality of US airlines. Baron (1969, 1974), McKenzie, *et al.* (1974) and Steuart (1974) analyze airline arrivals and departures. Figure 6.6 is adopted from Edwards and Newell (1969).

9   See Chin, *et al.* (1976). Diseconomies of scale exist whenever costs increase faster than size, that is, when the exponent on the size factor is greater than 1·0.

10 The major public reference on this is the study by de Neufville, *et al.* (1972). Numerous private studies, including those of the British Airports Authority, support its conclusions.

11 This formula, due to Steuart (1974), presumes that deviations from schedule are distributed exponentially, such that the standard deviation equals the square root of the mean. It then defines the number of positions required to meet all demands nineteen times out of twenty. McKenzie, *et al.* (1974) discusses other formulas by the Airborne Instruments Laboratory (1962), Mogligevsky (1965) and Stafford and Stafford (1969). The International Civil Aviation Organization recommends a similar procedure (ICAO Aerodrome Manual). Belshe (1971) did the study of San Francisco.

Chapter 7

1   Agee (1975) describes the American method of sizing airport
    terminals. The British Airports Authority is secretive about its
    approach, but does give details on the peak traffic patterns in
    its 1973/74 Annual Report.

2   Oliver and Samuel (1962) describe and illustrate the applica-
    tion of this concept of the behavior of service facilities. Newell
    (1971) gives a textbook presentation. This model may not
    provide absolutely accurate estimates of the delay of a system
    operating under stochastic loads when used with average rates
    of arrival, as Koopman (1972) shows. These errors apparently
    vanish, however, when the model is applied to a detailed
    description of the arrivals of the sort needed to carry out
    Koopman's analysis. Lee (1966) gives numerous examples of
    queues and delays at airports.

3   For example, the average waiting time for the use of a runway,
    W, is

$$W = \left(\frac{1}{1-r}\right)\left(\frac{r\lambda + \lambda\sigma^2}{2}\right)$$

where λ is the rate of arrivals and σ^2 is the variance of the
service rate. (The formula naturally only applies when the
service rate is greater than the average rate of arrivals.) Notice
that measures which reduce the variance of the service time
also reduce delays even when the degree of saturation, r, is
constant. See Odoni (1972).

4   McDonnell-Douglas Aircraft Company and Peat, Marwick and
    Mitchell carried out these analyses with the consulting advice
    of Horonjeff, who advocates the concept of absolute capacity.
    Horonjeff (1975) summarizes the available procedures for
    calculating capacity, which Peat, Marwick and Mitchell (1974)
    describe in detail, and which Hockaday and Kanafani (1974)
    demonstrate.

5   See US Department of Transportation, Federal Aviation
    Administration (1968) and Airborne Instruments Laboratory
    (1969 a,b) for details on the variations of the capacity of runways
    with different configurations and serving various types of air-
    craft.

6   Quoted from Horonjeff and Hoch (1975).

7   Carlin and Park (1970) document this phenomenon, using New
    York City's airports as an example.

8   This is a well-known economic principle, more generally refer-
    red to technically as the marginal cost pricing policy. This is

because, just as peak users who impose extra costs on the system should pay a surcharge, some users – such as those providing service to remote areas – provide net benefits to the system and should receive a discount. de Neufville and Mira (1974) apply this theory to airports and the air transport system. Little and McLeod (1972) discuss the practical aspects of peak-hour pricing at airports, and indicate how it was implemented at London/Heathrow. Fitzgerald and Aneuryn-Evans (1973) and Devanney (1975) trace out the long term implications of this policy for the financing of increases in capacity.

9   Yance (1971) describes the effect of quotas at Washington/ National in detail.

10   Stafford and Warskow (1961) provide a classic, if dated, example of how this might be done for a large-scale system such as a runway. Paullin and Horonjeff (1969) demonstrate how the same concepts could be applied more simply to a smaller system.

Chapter 8

1   de Neufville and Marks (1974) give some examples of this.

2   Foster (1975) discusses the weaknesses of the attempts to define a single criterion for evaluation, especially in his postscripts which extend and correct his earlier 1963 proposals.

3   Eads (1972) discusses these payments.

4   This restriction is contained in the Airport and Airways Development Act, Amendments of 1971. See US Congress, House Committee on Interstate and Foreign Commerce (1971).

5   See Doganis and Thompson (1973) for details.

6   Los Angeles has a unique program of buying up property within the most noisy areas. For London/Heathrow, a special regulation, UK (1966), permits the British Airports Authority to pay for insulating houses against noise. The limits on airline liability are set by the 1955 Hague Protocol to the Warsaw Convention, as further modified (due to public pressure in the United States) by the Montreal Agreement of 1958 which sets the higher limit for flights which start, end or make a scheduled stop in the United States. See Cheng (1962) or Seabrooke (1964) for a discussion of these conventions, copies of which are in Lowenfeld (1972).

7   ICAO (1970) provides worldwide data on this, and Doganis and Thompson (1973) present recent UK statistics.

8   For an example of this kind of promotion, see US FAA, Airports Service, Systems Planning Division (1967).

9 Typical arguments on this subject made by lobbyists representing special interests in air transport appear in the US DOT, Office of the Assistant Secretary for Policy and International Affairs (1973) and in many Congressional hearings, for example, US Congress, Senate Committee on Commerce, Subcommittee on Aviation (1969).

10 Quoted from the US Congress, House Committee on Interstate and Foreign Commerce, Subcommittee on Transportation and Aeronautics (1971); and from de Neufville and Yajima (1971) reprinted by the US Department of Transportation, Office of the Assistant Secretary for Policy and International Affairs (1972).

11 Berry (1967) did the classic study of this phenomenon.

12 UK CAA (1975a).

13 See Wilson (1966).

14 See Crowley (1973).

15 US Department of Transportation, Office of the Assistant Secretary for Policy and International Affairs (1972) tabulates aircraft and other costs. The UK Commission on the Third London Airport (1971) and Beesley (1973) discuss the value of time for air travelers, and US DOT (1970) gives data on airport delays.

16 The US National Transportation Safety Board (1972, 1973) publishes this information. For a more complete discussion, see US Congress, House Committee on Interstate and Foreign Commerce, Subcommittee on Transportation and Aeronautics (1970).

17 See US National Transportation Safety Board (1968).

18 See de Neufville and Stafford (1971) for further discussion of this point.

19 Horonjeff (1975) summarizes the prevalent American measures of noise, and the UK Committee on the Problem of Noise (1963) and the UK Noise Advisory Council (1972) discuss the British Noise and Number Index, the NNI. Galloway and Bishop (1970) discuss the worldwide evolution of noise indices.

20 UK Commission on the Third London Airport (1970) gives a detailed account, summarized by Flowerdew (1972) who also provides estimates of the total cost of noise.

21 The Hearings of the US Congress, House Committee on Science and Astronautics, Subcommittee on Aeronautics and Space Technology (1974) are a compendium of recent information on aircraft noise.

22 de Neufville and Marks (1974) review these procedures and illustrate their application through several case studies.

23 Stafford and Warskow (1961) illustrate how this can be done with airports, and Daellenbach (1974) and·Horonjeff (1962) implicitly use a cost-benefit approach to the problem of locating taxiways.

24 See Footnote 19, Chapter 3.

25 Mishan (1970).

26 Little and McLeod (1972).

27 See Footnote 8, Chapter 7.

28 This value is known as the opportunity cost of capital. Repeated studies confirm that it usually is over 10 percent. See de Neufville and Stafford (1971) and UK Cmnd. 3537.

29 ICAO (1966 and 1970) presents a rationale for this stance and Levine (1969) provides a critique. IATA (1973) tabulates the charges on aircraft operations throughout the world.

30 See UK Department of Trade and Industry (1963).

31 Yance (1971) discusses the effect of quotas at Washington/ National in detail.

32 See Footnote 10, Chapter 2.

References

Abbreviations used for Authors
CAA   Civil Aviation Authority
CAB   Civil Aeronautics Board
DOT   Department of Transportation
FAA   Federal Aviation Administration
IATA   International Air Transport Association
ICAO   International Civil Aviation Organization
PONYA   Port of New York Authority, now the Port Authority of New York and New Jersey.

Abbreviations used for Publishers and Journals
ASCE   American Society of Civil Engineers, 345 East 47th Street, New York, 10017.
GPO   Government Printing Office, Washington, DC.
HMSO   Her Majesty's Stationery Office, P.O. Box 569, London SE1 9NH.
ITTE   Institute of Transportation and Traffic Engineering, University of California, Berkeley, CA 94720.
JTEP   *Journal of Transport Economics and Policy.*
MIT   Massachusetts Institute of Technology, Cambridge, MA 02139.
NTIS   National Technical Information Service, Springfield, VA 22151.
TEJ   *Transportation Engineering Journal.*
TR   *Transportation Research*

Aéroport de Paris, Direction Générale, Relations Internationales, Section Etudes Statistiques (1974) *Statistiques de Trafic 1973*, Paris, April.

Agee, P. H. (1975) 'Air Terminal Planning – An Airline Industry View' in *Transportation Facilities Workshop: Passenger, Freight and Parking*, ASCE, pp. 335–357.

Airborne Instruments Laboratory (1969a) *Airport Capacity Handbook* (2nd Edition) AD 690 470, NTIS.

Airborne Instruments Laboratory (1969b) *Operational Development of Techniques for Computing Airport Capacity*, AD 690 477, NTIS.

Airborne Instruments Laboratory (1962) *Airport Terminal Plan Study*, RDS-136, US, FAA, Washington, DC.

Air Transport Association (Annual) *Air Transport Facts and Figures*, Washington, DC.

Aviation Week and Space Technology (1973) On-Time Performance Reports, Various Months.

Avril, P. (1969) *Politics in France*, Penguin, Harmondsworth, England and Baltimore, MD.

Ayres, R. U. (1969) *Technological Forecasting and Long-Range Planning*, McGraw-Hill, New York and Maidenhead.

Baram, M. S. (1974) 'Environmental Control of Construction Project Management', Reprinted in de Neufville and Marks (1974).

Baron, P. (1969) 'A Simulation Analysis of Airport Terminal Operations', *TR*, *3*, No. 4, December, pp. 481–491.

Baron, P. and Henning, D. (1974) 'The Passenger Terminal – A Systems Analysis Approach', *Airport Forum*, *4*, No. 2, pp. 69–82.

Bauml, S. (1974) Airport Revenues and Expenses, in Howard (1974), pp. 365–391

Beesley, M. E. (1973) *Urban Transport: Studies in Economic Policy*, Butterworth, London.

Belshe, R. D. (1971) 'A Study of Airport Terminal Gate Utilization', *Graduate Report*, *4*, ITTE.

Berry, B. J. L. (1967) *Geography of Market Centers and Retail Distribution*, Prentice-Hall, Englewood Cliffs, NJ and London.

Besse, G. and Desmas, G. (1966) *Forecasting for Air Transport – Methods and Results*, Study 66/7E (French Edition, 66/7F), Institut du Transport Aérien, Paris.

Blankenship, E. G. (1974) *The Airport; Architecture, Urban Integration, Ecological Problems*, Praeger, New York.

Block, J. (1975) 'Planning the Airport Environs – A European Viewpoint', *Proceedings ASCE Conference on International Air Transportation*, San Francisco, March, pp. 191–204.

Bovy, P. H. (1969) 'Ground Traffic at Major U.S. Airports', *Traffic Engineering and Control*, *11*, June, pp. 76–81.

Bower, L. L. (1974) *Elasticity of Air Travel Demand with Respect to Airport Access Cost*, Master of Science Thesis, George Washington University, Washington, DC.

British Airports Authority (Annual) *Reports and Accounts for the Year Ended 31st March*, London, June.

British Caledonian Airways, Ltd. (1975) *Statement in Support of Application 1A/20014/11 and 1A/20016/1 to Civil Aviation Authority*, London (Xerox).

Brown, J. F. (1965) 'Airport Accessibility Affects Passenger Development', *ASCE Journal of the Aero-Space Transport Division*, *91*, No. AT1, April, pp. 47–58.

Carlin, A. and Park, R. E. (1970) 'A Model of Long Delay at Busy Airports', *JTEP*, *4*, No. 1, January, pp. 37–54.

Cheng, B. (1962) *The Law of International Air Transport*, Stevens and Sons, London.

Chin, F., de Neufville, R. and Rebelo, J. (1976) 'Gate-Arrival Terminals – A Solution for Air Cargo?' *ASCE TEJ*, *102*, No. TE1, February, pp. 47–60.

Clawson, M. and Hall, P. (1973) *Planning and Urban Growth – An Anglo-American Comparison*, Johns Hopkins University Press, Baltimore, MD.

Cohen, S. S. (1969) *Modern Capitalist Planning: The French Model*, Weidenfeld and Nicholson, London.

Crowley, R. W. (1973). *A Case Study of the Effects of an Airport on Land Values*, *JTEP*, *7*, No. 2, May, pp. 144–152

Daellenbach, H. G. (1974) 'Dynamic Programming Model for Optimal Location of Runway Exits', *TR*, *8*, No. 3, August, pp. 225–232.

de Neufville, R. (1973) 'The Demand for Airport Access Services', *Traffic Quarterly*, *27*, No. 3, October, pp. 583–600, reprinted in de Neufville and Marks (1974).

de Neufville, R. and Keeney, R. L. (1974) 'Use of Decision Analysis in Airport Development for Mexico City', reprinted in de Neufville and Marks (1974).

de Neufville, R. and Keeney, R. L. (1973) 'Multiattribute Preference Analysis for Transportation Systems Evaluation', *TR*, *7*, No. 1, March, pp. 63–76.

de Neufville, R. and Marks, D. H. (1974) *Systems Planning and Design: Case Studies in Modeling, Optimization and Evaluation*, Prentice-Hall, Englewood Cliffs, NJ and London.

de Neufville, R. and Mierzejewski, E. (1972) 'Airport Access Cost-Effectiveness Analysis', *ASCE TEJ*, *98*, TE3, August, pp. 663–678. Reprinted in Howard (1974).

de Neufville, R. and Mira, L. J. (1974) 'Optimal Pricing Policies for Air Transport Networks', *TR*, *8*, No. 3, August, pp. 181–192.

de Neufville, R. and Stafford, J. (1971, 1974) *Systems Analysis for Engineers and Managers*, McGraw-Hill, New York and London, reprinted in the UK by McGraw-Hill and the Open University.

de Neufville, R. and Yajima, T. (1971) 'Economic Impact of Airport Development', *Transportation Research Forum Proceedings*, *12*, pp. 123–134.

de Neufville, R., Moore, H. M. III, and Yaney, J. (1972) *Optimal Use of Vehicular Systems in the Design of Airport Terminals*, Civil Engineering Systems Laboratory, MIT.

de Neufville, R., Skinner, R. and Koller, F. (1971) 'A Survey of the New York City Airport Limousine Service: A Demand Analysis', *Highway Research Record*, No. 348, pp. 192–201.

de Neufville, R., Wilson, N. H. M. and Fuertes, L. (1974) 'Consolidation of Urban Goods Movements: A Critical Analysis', *Transportation Research Record*, No. 496, pp. 16–27.

de Neufville, R. et al. (1972) *Access to Airports and Air Service*, PB 220 646/6, NTIS.

De Vany, A. S. and Garges, E. H. (1972) 'A Forecast of Air Travel and Airport and Airway Use in 1980', *TR*, *6*, No. 1, March.

Devanney, J. W., III and Tan, L. H. (1975) 'The Relationship between Short-Run Pricing and Investment Timing: The Port pricing and Expansion Example', *TR*, *9*, No. 6, December, pp. 329–337.

Doganis, R. S. and Thompson, G. F. (1973). *The Economics of British Airports*, Transport Studies Group, Department of Civil Engineering, Polytechnic of Central London.

Dolat, V. S., Koegler, J. C. and Nemeth, A. G. (1973) *Dual Lane Runway Study*, AD 762 462, NTIS.

Eads, G. C. (1972) *The Local Service Airline Experiment*, Brookings Institution, Washington, DC.

Edwards, J. W. and Newell, G. F. (1969) 'A Study of Gate Use at Honolulu International Airport', *Transportation Science*, *3*, No. 3, August, pp. 183–191.

Fitzgerald, E. V. K. and Aneuryn-Evans, G. B. (1973) 'The Economics of Airport Development and Control', *JTEP*, *7*, No. 3, September, pp. 1–4.

Flowerdew, A. D. J. (1972) 'The Cost of Airport Noise', *The Statistician*, *21*, No. 1, March, pp. 31–46.

Flughafen Zurich, Amt fuer Luftverkehr (1974) *Flughafen Zurich: Jahresbericht 1973*, April, Zurich.

Foster, C. D. (1975) *The Transport Problem* (2nd edition), Croom Helm, London.

France, Commissariat Général du Plan, Commission des Transports (1971) *Transports Aériens*, rapport du Comité du VI Plan, 1971–1975, Documentation Française, Paris.

Fruhan, W. E., Jr. (1972) *The Fight for Competitive Advantage*, Harvard Business School, Boston, MA.

Galloway, W. J. and Bishop, D. C. (1970) *Noise Exposure Forecasts: Evolution, Evaluation, Extensions and Land Use Interpretations*, AD 711 131, NTIS.

Gelerman, W. and de Neufville, R. (1973) 'Planning for Satellite Airports'. *ASCE TEJ*, *99*, No. TE3, August, pp. 537–551.

Genest, B.-A. (1970) *An Analysis of Accessibility Effects of Terminal Location and Configurations*, Doctoral Dissertation, Department of Civil Engineering, MIT.

Gordon, S. R. and de Neufville, R. (1975) *Rationalization of the European Air Net*, Department of Civil Engineering, MIT.

Gordon, S. R. and de Neufville, R. (1973) 'Design of Air Transportation Networks', *TR*, *7*, No. 3, September, pp. 207–222.

Haney, D. G. (1975) *Review of Aviation Forecasts and Forecasting Methodology*, US DOT, Assistant Secretary for Policy, Plans, and International Affairs, Office of Transportation Planning Analysis, Report DOT 40176–6, NTIS.

Hart, P. E. (1973) 'Population Densities and Optimal Aircraft Flight Paths', *Regional Studies*, *7*, No. 2, June, pp. 137–151.

Hockaday, S. L. M. and Kanafani, A. (1974) 'Developments in Airport Capacity Analysis', *TR*, *8*, No. 3, August, pp. 171–180.

Hooton, E. N., Burns, H. and Warskow, M. A. (1969) *Operational Development of Techniques for Computing Airport Capacity*, AD 690 477, NTIS.

Horonjeff, R. (1975) *Planning and Design of Airports* (2nd Edition), McGraw-Hill, New York and Maidenhead.

Horonjeff, R. (1962) 'Location and Number of Exit Taxiways', *ASCE Transactions*, *127*, Part IV, pp. 29–47.

Horonjeff, R. and Hoch, C. J. (1975) 'Some Facts About Horizontal Moving Sidewalks at Airports', in *Transportation Facilities Workshop: Passengers, Freight and Parking*, ASCE, pp. 323–334.

Howard, G. P. (1974), ed. *Airport Economic Planning*, MIT Press, Cambridge, MA and London.

Howard, G. P. and Augustinus, J. G. (1974) 'Market Research and Forecasting for the Airport Market', in Howard (1974), pp. 109–127.

Howrey, E. P. (1969) 'On the Choice of Forecasting Models for Air Travel', *Journal of Regional Science*, 9, No. 2, August, pp. 215–224.

Hurst, F. (1974) 'Public Parking at Port Authority Airports', in Howard (1974), pp. 231–244.

IATA (Various Dates and Amendments), *Airport Terminal Reference Manual*, 5th Edition, Montreal.

IATA (1973) *User Charges Manual*, Geneva.

IATA, Airports Terminals Advisory Committee (1975) *Capacity Evaluation Studies Airport Terminal Facilities*, Montreal (mimeo).

ICAO (Various Dates) *Aerodrome Manual*, Parts 1 to 7 and Annex 14, Multiple Editions, DOC 7920 – AN/865, Montreal and HMSO.

ICAO (Annual) *Traffic*, Montreal and HMSO.

ICAO (1972) *Manual on Air Traffic Forecasting*, DOC 8991–AT/722, Montreal and HMSO.

ICAO (1970) *Development of Airport Revenues from Non-Aeronautical Sources (Concessions, Rentals and Free Zones)*, Circular 101-AT/22, Montreal.

ICAO (1969) *Airport Master Planning*, DOC 8769–AN/891, Montreal and HMSO.

ICAO (1966) *ICAO's Policies on Taxation in the Field of International Air Transport*, DOC 8632-C/968, November, Montreal.

Jantsch, E. (1967) *Technological Forecasting in Perspective*, Organization for Economic Co-Operation and Development, Paris.

Jego, R. (1975) *Competition Between Air and Rail Service in the Boston-New York Corridor*, Master of Science Thesis, Department of Aeronautics and Astronautics, MIT.

Kiernan, J. D. (1970) *A Survey and Assessment of Air Travel Forecasting*, Report AD 705 121, NTIS.

Knudsen, T. (1976) *Uncertainties in Airport Cost Analysis and Their Effect on Site Selections*, Doctoral Dissertation, ITTE.

Koopman, B. O. (1972) 'Air Terminal Queues under Time-Dependent Conditions', *Operations Research*, 20, No. 6, November–December, pp. 1089–1114.

Lee, A. M. (1966) *Applied Queuing Theory*, Macmillan, London and St. Martin's Press, New York.

Levine, M. E. (1969) 'Landing Fees and the Airport Congestion Problem', *Journal of Law and Economics*, *12*, No. 1, April, pp. 79–108.

Little, I. M. D. and McLeod, K. M. (1972) 'New Pricing Policy for British Airports', *JTEP*, *6*, No. 2, May, pp. 101–115.

Los Angeles International Airport (1975) *10-Year Summary of Air Traffic*, 1965–1974, mimeo.

Lowenfeld, A. F. (1972) *Aviation Law Cases and Materials*, Matthew Bender and Co., New York.

Manheim, M. L. (1974) 'Reaching Decisions About Technological Projects with Social Consequences: A Normative Model', reprinted in de Neufville and Marks (1974).

Martino, J. P. (1972) *Technological Forecasting for Decision Making*, American Elsevier, New York, and Elsevier, Amsterdam.

Massé, P. (1965) *Le Plan ou l'Anti-Hazard*, Gallimard, Paris.

Mayerson, M. and Banfield, E. C. (1955) *Politics, Planning and the Public Interest*, Free Press, Glencoe, IL.

McKenzie, A. J., Huggett, J. W. E. and Ogden, K. W. (1974) 'Staging of Improvements to Air Transport Terminals', *ASCE TEJ*, *100*, No. TE4, November, pp. 855–872.

Merewitz, L. (1973) 'How do Rapid Transit Projects Compare in Cost-Estimating Experience?' *Proceedings of the First International Conference on Transportation Research*, Bruges, Belgium, June, pp. 485–493.

Mishan, E. J. (1970) 'What is Wrong with Roskill?' *JTEP*, *4*, No. 3, September, pp. 221–234.

Mogligevsky, D. A. (1965). *Siting and Design of Airports* (English Translation), AD 622 357, NTIS.

Moore, H. L., III (1973) *Forecasting Demand at Airports*, Civil Engineer Thesis, Department of Civil Engineering, MIT.

Newell, G. F. (1971) *Applications of Queuing Theory*, Chapman and Hall, London and Barnes and Noble, Boston.

Odoni, A. (1972) An Airport Capacity Analysis Overview, in Dolat, Koegler and Nemeth (1973).

Oliver, R. M. and Samuel, A. H. (1962) 'Reducing Letter Delays in Post Offices', *Operations Research*, *10*, No. 6, November–December, pp. 839–892

Park, R. E. (1966) 'Airport Accessibility and Detroit Passengers', *ASCE Journal of Aero-Space Transport Division*, *92*, No. AT2, November, pp. 65–81.

Parry, G. (1969) *British Government*, Butterworth, London.

R. M. Parsons Co. and Air Transportation Association of America (1973) *The Apron-Terminal Complex – Analysis of Concepts for Evaluation of Terminal Buildings*, AD 771 186/4GI, NTIS.

Paullin, R. L. and Horonjeff, R. (1969) 'Sizing of Departure Lounges in Airport Buildings', *ASCE TEJ*, *95*, TE2, May, pp. 267–278.

Peat, Marwick, Mitchell Co. and McDonnell-Douglas Aircraft Co. (1974) *Airfield Capacity and Delay Handbook*, Report FAA-RD-74-124. Prepared for the US FAA, Washington, DC.

Port Authority of New York and New Jersey (Annual) *Aviation Statistics*, New York.

Port Authority of New York and New Jersey, Aviation Economics Department (1974) *Airport Statistics Through December 1973*, New York.

PONYA (1965) *New York's Domestic Air Passenger Market, April 63– March 64*, New York.

PONYA, Aviation Department, Aviation Economics Division (1970) *Market Research and Forecasting for the Airport Market*, (mimeo), New York.

PONYA, Aviation Department, Forecast and Analysis Division (1958) *Forecast of Overseas Passenger Market Through New York 1965–1975*, New York.

PONYA, Aviation Department, Forecast and Analysis Division (1957) *Air Travel Forecasting Market Analysis Method, Domestic Air Passenger Market, 1965–1975*, Eno Foundation, Saugatuck, CT.

PONYA, Department of Airport Development, Airport Planning Bureau (1950) *Air Traffic Forecast, New York – New Jersey Port District 1950–1980*, New York.

Rittel, H. and Webber, M. (1973) 'Dilemmas in a General Theory of Planning', *Policy Sciences*, *4*, No. 2, June, pp. 155–170.

Rose, R. (1969) ed. *Policy-Making in Britain – a Reader in Government*, Macmillan, London.

Rusconi-Clerici, I. (1976) *Are Airport Planners Forgetting About Transfers?* Master of Science Thesis, Department of Civil Engineering, MIT.

Russell, A. F. D. and O'Flaherty, C. A. (1969) 'Motor Vehicles at European Airports', *Traffic Engineering and Control, 11*, in 3 parts, July, pp. 13–134; August, pp. 189–192; September, pp. 238–244.

Seabrooke, G. A. (1964) *Air Law*, University of London Press, London.

Shonfield, A. (1965) *Modern Capitalism – The Changing Balance of Public and Private Power*, Oxford University Press, London and New York.

Simi, F. and Bankir, J. (1968) *Avant et Après Concorde*, Editions du Seuil, Paris.

Sommer, R. (1974) *Tight Spaces: Hard Architecture and How to Humanize It*, Prentice-Hall, Englewood Cliffs, NJ and London.

Stafford, P. H. and Stafford, D. L. (1969) 'Space Criterion for Aircraft Aprons', *ASCE TEJ, 95*, No. TE2, May, pp. 237–243.

Stafford, P. H. and Warskow, M. A. (1961) 'Airport Design by Economic Analysis', *ASCE Journal of the Air Transport Division, 87*, No. AT2, August, pp. 29–53.

Steuart, G. N. (1974) 'Gate Position Requirements at Metropolitan Airports', *Transportation Science, 8*, No. 2, May, pp. 169–189.

Stratford, A. H. (1973) *Air Transport Economics in the Supersonic Era* (2nd Edition), Macmillan, London and St. Martin's Press, New York.

Sutherland, R. J., Chairman, Committee on Transportation to and from Airports of the Technical Council on Urban Transportation (1969) 'Survey of Ground-Access Problems at Airports', *ASCE TEJ, 95*, TE1, February, pp. 115–142.

Systems Analysis and Research Corporation (1968) *The Growth of Air Commerce in Areas Served by San Francisco and Oakland International Airports*, SC-645-68, August, Cambridge, MA.

Tilles, R. (1973) 'Curb Space at Airport Terminals', *Traffic Quarterly, 27*, No. 3, October, pp. 563–582.

UK (1966) *The London (Heathrow) Airport Noise Insulation Grants Scheme 1966*, HMSO.

UK, CAA (1975a) *The Development of the UK Airport System*, CAP 372, London.

UK, CAA (1975b) *Airport Development in the Central England Area*, CAP 373, London.

UK, CAA (1975c) *Future Airport Development in the Northern Regions*, CAP 374, London.

UK, CAA (1972) *Airport Planning: An Approach on a National Basis,* London.

UK, Cmnd. 4899 (1972) *Civil Aviation Policy Guidance,* HMSO.

UK, Cmnd. 4213 (1969) *Civil Aviation Policy,* HMSO.

UK, Cmnd. 3437 (1967) *Nationalized Industries: A Review of Economic and Financial Objectives,* HMSO.

UK, Commission on the Third London Airport (1971) *Report,* HMSO.

UK, Commission on the Third London Airport (1970) *Papers and Proceedings,* HMSO.

UK, Committee on the Problem of Noise (1963, reprinted 1973) *Noise – Final Report,* (Cmnd. 2056, The 'Wilson Report'), HMSO.

UK, Department of Trade (1976) *Airport Strategy for Great Britain, Part 2: Regional Airports,* HMSO.

UK, Department of Trade (1975) *Airport Strategy for Great Britain Part 1: The London Area,* HMSO.

UK, Department of Trade and Industry (1973) *Action Against Noise – Progress Report 1973,* HMSO.

UK, Ministry of Transport (1970) *Report of a Study of Rail Links with Heathrow Airport,* HMSO.

UK, Noise Advisory Council (1972) *Aircraft Noise: Should the Noise and Number Index be Revised?,* HMSO.

UK, Noise Advisory Council (1971) *Aircraft Noise: Flight Routing Near Airports,* HMSO.

US, CAB (Quarterly) *Origin-Destination Survey of Airline Passenger Traffic,* GPO.

US, CAB and FAA (Semiannual) *Airport Activity Statistics of Certificated Route Air Carriers,* GPO.

US Congress (1970) *Airport and Airway Development Act,* Public Law 91-258, GPO.

US Congress, House Committee on Interstate and Foreign Commerce (1969) *Aviation Facilities Maintenance and Development,* Part 1, Hearings 91–22, July–September, GPO.

US Congress, House Committee on Interstate and Foreign Commerce, Subcommittee on Transportation and Aeronautics (1971) *Airport and Airway Trust Fund,* Hearings 92–35, June, GPO.

US Congress, House Committee on Interstate and Foreign Commerce, Subcommittee on Transportation and Aeronautics (1970)

Aviation Safety and Aircraft Piracy, Hearings 91–85, February 1969 and December 1970, GPO.

US Congress, House Committee on Science and Astronautics, Subcommittee on Aeronautics and Space Technology (1974) *Aircraft Noise Abatement*, Hearings No. 44, July, GPO.

US Congress, Senate Committee on Commerce, Subcommittee on Aviation (1975) *Adequacy of Air Service in Illinois*, Hearings 93-130, July 1974, GPO.

US Congress, Senate Committee on Commerce, Subcommittee on Aviation (1973) *Local Air Service to Small Communities*, Hearings 92-102, April, GPO.

US Congress, Senate Committee on Commerce, Subcommittee on Aviation (1970) *Local Air Service to Small Communities*, Hearings 91-100, April–August, GPO.

US Congress, Senate Committee on Commerce, Subcommittee on Aviation (1969) *Airport/Airways Development*, Hearings 91–13, June–July, GPO.

US Congress, Senate Committee on Commerce, Subcommittee on Aviation (1965) *Adequacy of Trunkline Air Service to Medium Sized Intermediate Cities*, Hearings 89–26, July, GPO.

US, Department of Commerce, Civil Aeronautics Commission (1950) *Airport Terminal Activities and Space Utilization*, GPO.

US, DOT (1974) *1974 National Transportation Report – Current Performance and Future Prospects*, December, Washington, DC.

US, DOT (1970) *Terminal Area Airline Delay Data, 1964–1969*, September, Washington, DC.

US, DOT, FAA (1974) *Statistical Handbook of Aviation, Calendar Year 1973*, GPO.

US, DOT, FAA (1973) *National Airport System Plan*, GPO.

US, DOT, FAA (1971) *Airport Master Plans*, GPO.

US, DOT, FAA (1968) *Airport Capacity Criteria Used in Preparing the National Airport Plan*, AC 150/5060-1A, Washington, DC.

US, DOT, FAA and Airport Operators Council International (1970) *Planning the Metropolitan Airport System*, AC 150/5070-5, GPO.

US, DOT, FAA, Office of Aviation Economics, Aviation Forecast Division (Annual) *Aviation Forecasts*, Washington, DC.

US, DOT, FAA, Office of Aviation Economics, Aviation Forecast Division (Semiannual) *Profiles of Scheduled Air Carrier Operations – Top 100 US Airports*, GPO.

US, DOT, Office of the Assistant Secretary for Policy and International Affairs, Office of Policy Review (1973) *Aviation Cost Allocation Study Working Paper 16: View of the Users*, April, Washington, DC.

US, DOT, Office of the Assistant Secretary for Policy and International Affairs, Office of Policy Review (1972) *Aviation Cost Allocation Study Working Paper 9: Benefits*, October, Washington, DC.

US, FAA, Airports Service, Systems Planning Division (1967) *The Airport – Its Influence on the Community Economy*, GPO.

US, FAA, Bureau of Facilities and Materiel, Airports Division (1960) *Airport Terminal Buildings*, GPO.

US, FAA, Bureau of National Capital Airports (1962) *Aviation Forecasts for Dulles International Airport and Washington National Airport, 1963–1967*, Washington, DC.

US, National Transportation Safety Board (1973) *A Preliminary Analysis of Aircraft Accident Data – US Civil Aviation 1972*, NTSB-APA-73-1, April, Washington, DC.

US, National Transportation Safety Board (1972) *A Study of the US Air Carrier Accidents 1964–1969*, NTSB-AAS-72-5, May, Washington, DC.

US, National Transportation Safety Board (1968) *An Analysis of Aircraft Accident Data – US General Aviation*, (mimeo), Washington, DC.

Voorhees, A. M. (1966) 'Airport Access, Circulation and Parking', *ASCE Journal of Aero-Space Transport Division*, *92*, AT1, January, pp. 63–75.

Webber, M. (1973) 'On the Technics and Politics of Transport Planning', *Working Paper 219*, Institute of Urban and Regional Development, University of California, Berkeley, CA.

Wheatcroft, S. (1956) *The Economics of European Air Transport*, Manchester University Press, Manchester.

Whitlock, E. M. and Cleary, E. F. (1969) 'Planning Ground Transportation Facilities for Airports', *Highway Research Record*, No. 274, pp. 1–13.

Whitlock, E. M. and Sanders, D. B. (1974) 'Systems Analysis of Ground Transportation at Major US Airports', *Transportation Research Record*, No. 499, pp. 58–69.

Wilson, A. (1973). *The Concorde Fiasco*, Penguin Books, Harmondsworth, England and Baltimore, MD.

Wilson, G. W., et al. (1966) *The Impact of Highway Investment in Development*, Brookings Institution, Washington, DC.

Yance, J. V. (1971) 'Airline Demand for Use of an Airport and Airport Rents', *TR*, *5*, No. 4, December, pp. 267–281.

Young, C. S. and Nemec, J., Jr. (1974) 'Systems Analysis in Airport Master Planning', *ASCE TEJ*, *100*, TE4, November, pp. 933–941.

Index